Principles

M000203133

in a Nutshell

Principles of Economics in a Nutshell provides a succinct overview of contemporary economic theory. This key text introduces economics as a social science, presenting the discipline as an evolving field shaped within historical context rather than a fixed set of ideas.

Chapters on microeconomics introduce concepts of scarcity and tradeoffs, market analysis (the Marshallian cross of supply and demand) and the theory of the firm and market structure. Chapters on macroeconomics begin with an explanation of national income accounting, followed by discussions of macroeconomic theory in the goods market and in the money market from both a Keynesian and Classical view. The text concludes with examples of how to expand upon core material, introducing the perspectives of feminist and ecological economics.

This book will be of great importance to students new to economics and is ideal for use on single-semester Principles courses or as a primer on economics courses in other settings. The text is fully supported by online resources, which include a set of analytical questions and suggestions for further reading for each chapter.

Lorenzo Garbo is Professor in the Department of Economics at University of Redlands, USA.

Dorene Isenberg is Professor in the Department of Economics at University of Redlands, USA.

Nicholas Reksten is Assistant Professor in the Department of Economics at University of Redlands, USA.

"This introductory economics textbook is long overdue. For too long, students taking their first economics course have had difficulty seeing how material can be used to address the most important issues we face in society. This textbook gives students a strong foundation in economic theory *and* shows them how to use what they learn to address interesting and relevant topics in economics such as non-market transactions, household production and environmental problems."

– Professor Matthew Lang, University of California, Riverside

"This textbook is for professors who want to teach the basics of economics within a broad and open-minded Liberal Arts framework."

– Professor James Devine, Loyola Marymount University

"A much-needed alternative textbook to engage students in today's economic issues."

– Professor Mark Maier, Glendale Community College

Principles
of Economics
in a Nutshell

Lorenzo Garbo, Dorene Isenberg,
and Nicholas Reksten

Routledge
Taylor & Francis Group

LONDON AND NEW YORK

First published 2020
by Routledge
2 Park Square, Milton Park, Abingdon, Oxon OX14 4RN

and by Routledge
52 Vanderbilt Avenue, New York, NY 10017

Routledge is an imprint of the Taylor & Francis Group, an informa business

British Library Cataloguing-in-Publication Data
A catalogue record for this book is available from the British Library

Library of Congress Cataloging-in-Publication Data
Names: Garbo, Lorenzo, author. | Isenberg, Dorene, 1949- author. | Reksten, Nicholas, author.
Title: Principles of economics in a nutshell / Lorenzo Garbo, Dorene Isenberg and Nicholas Reksten.
Description: Abingdon, Oxon; New York, NY: Routledge, 2020.
  | Includes bibliographical references and index.
Identifiers: LCCN 2019048044 (print) | LCCN 2019048045 (ebook)
  | ISBN 9780367321208 (hbk) | ISBN 9780367321192 (pbk)
  | ISBN 9780429316739 (ebk)
Subjects: LCSH: Economics.
Classification: LCC HB75 .G315 2020 (print) | LCC HB75 (ebook)
  | DDC 330--dc23
LC record available at https://lccn.loc.gov/2019048044
LC ebook record available at https://lccn.loc.gov/2019048045

ISBN: 978-0-367-32120-8 (hbk)
ISBN: 978-0-367-32119-2 (pbk)
ISBN: 978-0-429-31673-9 (ebk)

Typeset in Avenir, Minion and Trade Gothic
by Servis Filmsetting Ltd, Stockport, Cheshire

Visit the eResources: www.routledge.com/9780367321192

Contents

Figures

All figures have been created by the authors for the purposes of this work.

Tables

Preface

We set out to write this brief volume on introductory economics in the hope that we could use our combined 60 years of teaching experience to create a text that would fit well with a one-semester principles course that combined macro- and microeconomics, like ours, in which the instructor was eager to supplement the textbook with up-to-date outside sources. Too often, we found textbooks to be bloated with unnecessary material that we had to ask students to read around and that were, as a result, too expensive. We felt that students could benefit from concise, straightforward presentations of the theoretical material that would leave plenty of room for the discussion of applications and extensions in the classroom. Using a draft of this work with our students confirmed that this approach could be effective in teaching introductory economics, and, indeed, that it would be superior to other, more traditional methods of introducing the subject.

Additionally, we had long realized that economics is a discipline badly in need of updating the ways in which introductory courses are approached. Much of this we had been trying in our individual courses. Rather than teach economics as a dogmatic, abstract, and distant discipline, we wanted to ground it in its history for students, showing them how it emerged and emphasizing that it is a living subject, with arguments and divergent views. We wanted to demonstrate to students that they could use the foundational models presented here as a bridge to explore other questions and schools of thought. We hope that using this text inspires students, especially those who may not have traditionally studied the subject, to take other courses in economics. We were all drawn to the subject, at least in part, because of its powerful potential to explain the world and solve social problems.

The book begins by introducing economics as a social science and explaining its historical roots, discussing especially the work of Adam Smith and John Maynard Keynes, arguably the two most important figures in the founding of modern economics. Next, it discusses the concepts of scarcity and tradeoffs in order to explore how societies might make decisions regarding resource use. The microeconomics portion of the text introduces the concept of markets, including the Marshallian cross supply-and-demand framework, different types of competition, market failures, and an analysis of supply decisions by firms. The macroeconomics portion begins by introducing a flow model of the macroeconomy and foundational concepts of national income accounting, and potential macroeconomic goals, such as GDP growth, price stability, and reduced unemployment. It then introduces the competing macroeconomic paradigms of the Classical and Keynesian models, first in the goods market and then incorporating money and the banking system into the analysis. The final chapter of the book introduces the feminist and ecological economics schools of thought in order to demonstrate possible extensions of the models discussed in the text along with further questions that students may explore within the introductory course and elsewhere.

1
More than just the stock market

Introduction to economics

 ## 1.1 Economics as a social science

Social science, according to the Oxford Dictionary, is *the scientific study of human society and social relationships*. The traditional social sciences are: anthropology, economics, politics, psychology, and sociology; more recently, interdisciplinary fields such as women's, gender, and sexuality studies, race and ethnic studies, humanitarian affairs, and so on, have been added to the more traditional list.

What distinguishes *economics* among these social sciences? The noun *economics* comes from the Greek *oikos-nomia*, which became *oeconomia* in Latin. *Nomia* in Greek means "distribution, arrangement, management" (think also about: astro*nomy*, agro*nomy* ...), while *oikos* means "household". Thus, *economics* originally meant "management of the household, of the place we live in". This is a definition worth reflecting upon for a moment, as it may help you distinguish economics from adjacent fields of study: for instance, you may want to consider the fact that "management of the household" does not only imply making the household wealthier. Also, the emphasis of this definition falls on the household as a whole, and not on its individual components. This is quite different from what we experience in our highly individualistic society! In ancient Greece, the purpose of human existence was the enjoyment of a *good life*, and such an objective could only be attained within the community, that is, the *polis* (city-state). It was the community – and not the individual – that could achieve good social results, a prerequisite for well-being. Therefore, individuals were to conceive their conduct in economic affairs in light of their relations with each other and so with the community of citizens on which they depended. Here is how Aristotle (384–322 BCE) wrote about it in *Politics*:

> Man is by nature a political animal. And therefore, men, even when they do not require one another's help, desire to live together; they are also brought together by their common interests in proportion as they severally

attain to any measure of well-being. This is certainly the chief end, both of individuals and of states. (III, 6)

Seeing then that the state is made up of households, before speaking of the state we must speak of the management of the household. ... And there is another element of a household, the so-called art of getting wealth [*chrematistike*], which, according to some, is identical with household management, according to others, a principal part of it. (I, 3)

More than two millennia have gone by since then, and you may think that many aspects of human and social existence have changed. You may think, for instance, that today we are much less dependent on others in the pursuit of our own well-being (*individualism*). But ... are we really? Where do you stand in regard to the possibility for human beings to achieve well-being *un*-collectively?

Let's reflect further on the definition of economics given earlier, which may be rephrased as: economics deals with the use of the resources of the household with the objective of producing the greatest well-being for the household itself. A simple generalization of "household" to whatever environment we live in updates the definition of economics to a concept we can relate to more easily: the management of resources of a city, a state, a country, and so on, with the objective of maximizing the overall well-being of the corresponding population. This is where troubles begin: is there a unique definition of the well-being of a community, a definition we could all agree upon? And even if we could agree to consider *just one* definition of the well-being of a community, how likely is it that we would also agree on how and what to measure in order to evaluate it? How likely is it that we would also agree on what policies or strategies would improve it the most? Even people with fairly similar visions of the world are unlikely to share the same idea of well-being, to choose the same unit of measure and techniques in order to evaluate it, to imagine the same policies to improve it. Economists generally agree that the purview of economics is the management of resources with the objective of maximizing the overall well-being of the community, but often disagree –like everybody else – on the practical, concrete translation of the community's well-being, on what and how to measure it, and on what to do in order to improve it. The next section of this chapter will provide you with some help in rationalizing the most common causes of divergence of opinion among economists.

Before we get there, though, let's do some more work on our definition. Given the inclusion of economics among the social *sciences*, the study of the management of resources for the well-being of the community must be conducted according to the methods and principles of *science*: it has to be a systematic and methodical study. Again, *scientific* comes from the Latin *scientia*, which means *knowledge*, and *scientific* then means *productive of knowledge*. How does one then approach the study of economics according to a scientific method?

Francis Bacon, a British philosopher, in 1620 published a treatise entitled *Instauratio Magna*, which contains the very first full and modern description of the *scientific method* (Bacon in fact became later known as the *founder* of the scientific method). In its most basic form, such method consists of a strict sequence of methodological steps, that can be summarized as follows:

1. faithful record of natural phenomena;
2. derivation of aphorisms – system-free inferences of/from what one observed;
3. "negative instances" are used to eliminate faulty aphorisms, while aphorisms that are not negated by experimentation are gathered into generalizations that constitute "knowledge."

A couple of examples should clarify.

*   Example 1: a truthful aphorism
    *   I observe water running through my bare fingers and wetting them.
    *   I derive the aphorism that when water runs through my bare fingers, my fingers get wet.
    *   Are there instances in which this does not happen, that can negate my aphorism? No.
    *   Thus, I can generalize and say that water wets bare fingers.

*   Example 2: a faulty aphorism
    *   I observe that during a downturn of the economy (recession) there are more poor people around.
    *   I make the inference (aphorism) that during a recession people become poorer.
    *   Are there instances that deny my inference? Yes: during the last recession, for instance, the average compensation of CEOs increased.
    *   My aphorism is faulty.

Summarizing, the conceptual sequence of the scientific method – and so also of economic analysis – consists therefore of: facts → theory → check of the validity of the theory against facts.

1.2 On the scientific character of economics, ideology, and perspectives

In the previous section we have already come across some causes of disagreement among economists. There is more. We just saw that economics, as a social *science*, follows the *scientific method*: there is fundamental agreement on that; but how *scientific* can economics really be? Can the study of economics, which has so much to do with the human experience and understanding of reality, the types of interactions, norms, structure of society, historical patterns, and so on, lead to *scientific* knowledge? Joan Robinson, a celebrated British economist, in *Freedom and Necessity* (1970, p. 119) wrote: "The methods to which the natural sciences owe their success – controlled experiment and exact observation of continually recurring phenomena – cannot be applied to the study of human beings by human beings." Even if economists faithfully apply the scientific method, the outcome of their work may have to be taken differently from, say, the outcome of a chemical reaction that can be repeated *ad infinitum* in the same exact conditions. Thus, Robinson concludes that, "The function of social science is quite different from that of the natural sciences – it is to provide society with an organ of self-consciousness." What could that mean?

The degree of certainty with which economists perceive the outcome of their work (that is, how *scientific* economists consider the outcomes of their work) tend to divide economists into different camps: it typically distinguishes scholars who self-identify as *economists* or as *political economists*, depending on whether the focus of their work and their vision of the discipline are restricted to what can be objectively measured (*pure* economic relationships), or whether they can only conceive economic relationships in contextual ways, within the political, historical, cultural, and social framework in which economic relationships take place.[1] Of course, the question of whether anything at all can be measured truly objectively remains open.

An additional and growing area of disagreement among economists has to do with the system of beliefs and moral values (*ideologies*) scholars abide by. The impact of ideology on one's approach can be best appreciated through examples. Consider, for instance, the following passage, taken from Sismondi's "On the Condition of the Work People in Manufactories" (1847 [1834], p. 196):

> The most important of all questions in Political Economy [is] the share of happiness which wealth ought to diffuse among those who contribute by their labour to its creation. With us it is a fixed principle that social order ought never to sacrifice one class of men to another, and that, whilst admitting divers conditions, poor as well as rich, these differences are only

protected for the common welfare of all, this inequality is only legitimate, because it secures, even to the humblest, a portion of comfort, which he could not find in savage life.

You may be convinced that some degree of economic inequality is necessary to maintain incentives for improvement, innovation; but can the degree of economic inequality become excessive? Would someone who holds beliefs similar to Sismondi's, advocate for some form of redistribution of wealth (or income) from the higher to the lower economic echelons of society? Do you think that economic rights are fundamental human rights? Can you imagine someone holding a different set of beliefs?

Or consider the following statement by John Stuart Mill (1848, pp. 364–5), one of the most important philosophers and political economists of the nineteenth century:

Everyone has a right to live. We will suppose this granted. But no one has the right to bring creatures into life, to be supported by other people. ... If a man cannot support even himself unless others help him, those others are entitled to say that they do not also undertake the support of any off-spring which it is physically possible for him to summon into the world. ... It would be possible for the state to guarantee employment at ample wages to all who are born. But if it does this, it is bound in self-protection, and for the sake of every purpose for which government exists, to provide that no person shall be born without its consent.

Do you share this ideology? Would someone who holds these beliefs advocate for a policy of taxation of the wealthy and subsidization of the poor? Of the children of the very poor?

Political or religious ideologies inform our moral priorities, determine what we think could and could not be infringed, and thus differentiate among the possible policies and strategies economists envision with the objective to increase the overall well-being of society. Most people, for instance, think that private property is sacred, and may think that taxation of one's lawfully earned income is an infringement of the fundamental right to private property. In addition, taxation may decrease the incentive to improve one's economic condition and may thus diminish buoyant economic perspectives for the whole country. We would all suffer from this, one would say. But when we see a growing, often mentally ill, homeless population on the streets of one of the wealthiest countries in the world, or full-time salaries that may be insufficient to put enough food on the table, we may want to consider whether there is a more fundamental right that would be infringed by not using some taxation to alleviate the suffering of a portion of the population.

Finally, economists may also disagree because they structure their reasoning on the basis of different *economic paradigms* or *schools of thought*, where paradigms are understood as "systems of thought" or "economic theories" that include the specific questions economists try to answer, what facts, institutions, and behaviors they consider as assumptions of their thought process, and the methodology followed in the development of their theories. Paradigms can be motivated by history, intellectual/scientific evolution, ideology, or by any conceivable combinations of the above, and thus you may have that a later paradigm completely supersedes a previous one (for instance, think about the effect of the Copernican Revolution, which moved us from the Ptolemaic paradigm – the sun rotates around the earth – to the Copernican paradigm – the earth revolves around the sun), or coexisting paradigms, that is, alternative ways in which phenomena can be approached, studied, improved upon. Two coexisting paradigms in the study of economics, for instance, have to do with believing that "supply creates demand" (a.k.a. Say's Law) or that "demand creates supply". To see how these two paradigms can lead to disagreement among economists, imagine that two economists are asked to figure out how to increase the level of income of a country. Assume that the first economist abides by the paradigm that by incentivizing the production of goods you automatically also create the demand (the purchase) of the additional goods produced: in the most simplistic terms, this would be because when firms increase the production of goods they will have to hire more workers and thus pay more salaries, and those additional salaries will end up being spent on the additional goods produced. The second economist instead believes that it is the population's willingness and ability to purchase additional goods that need to be incentivized first because it is the additional "demand" of goods that will then make firms produce more goods, as firms will see the opportunity to make more profits and will go for it. You can then easily imagine that these two economists will end up with very different recommendations on how to increase the level of income of the country: the first, for instance, may want to decrease taxes on firms so that firms have an incentive to produce more; the second may want the government to spend more on, say, infrastructure, in order to kickstart the process on the demand side of the economy.

As you embark in the study of economics, you are likely to find some reference to the following three fundamental paradigms: the *orthodox* paradigm, also known as the mainstream or traditional paradigm, which includes theories built on the basis of the existence of competitive markets; the *Marxian* paradigm, in which competitive markets are seen as a particular way, prevalent in a specific historical time-period, in which the economy is organized, and thus focuses on the evolution of the ways in which economies operate or can operate; and finally the *institutionalist* paradigm, that leads to theories of the economy based on the role and power of institutions in economic affairs.

Several other paradigms arose during the twentieth century and continue to arise from various critiques, modifications, and crosspollinations of these three general schools of thought. Among them, of increasing importance are the *feminist* and the *ecological* paradigms, which will be introduced at the end of this chapter and further explored in Chapter 8.

▮ 1.3 Concept of economic system

The general definition of economics given earlier in this chapter referred to the study of the management of resources in the environment we live in, say, the country, with the objective of maximizing the overall well-being of the population. This definition was famously restated by Lionel Robbins, a British economist, in his *An Essay on the Nature and Significance of Economic Science* (1932, p. 16); there, we read:

> Economics is the science which studies human behaviour as a relationship between ends and scarce means which have alternative uses.

According to this definition, economics studies more or less broad aspects of the ways in which human beings organize themselves to use the resources they have to satisfy their needs and wants. The adjective "scarce" that accompanies "resources" in Robbins' definition is very important here: "scarce" refers to the fact that the resources taken into account in economics have to be in *limited, finite* supply. Thus, economists do not concern themselves at all with resources that are infinitely available (say, air).

The specific way in which human beings organize themselves to use scarce resources to satisfy their needs and wants is referred to as an *economic system*. More precisely, then, an economic system consists of:

1. methods of production: inputs, a.k.a. factors of production (such as labor, primary resources, machinery, and so on), and the technologies utilized in the various production processes;
2. customary and legal processes that determine the payments to the factors of production (e.g., wages as payment to labor; profits as payment to the owners of capital; rents as payment to the owners of land);
3. modalities in which distribution of what is produced occurs (markets, gifts, centralized allocation by the government, and so on);
4. modes of utilization of what is produced: determinants and patterns of consumption.

Modes of production, compensation, distribution, and consumption (that is, economic systems) inevitably reflect the evolution of societies, knowledge, moral values, cultural norms, and so on. Thus, at any given time many economic systems coexist in the world, while each economic system continuously reflects social, legal, scientific changes, and thus is rarely static. For instance, think about the impact that the internet is currently having on our own economic system: cyber-commuting, crowdfunding, digital deliveries, and so on, were all unthinkable only a few years ago, and are clearly modifying the ways in which we produce, compensate factors of production, distribute, and consume.

Past economic systems are typically the object of study of *economic history*, *history of economic thought*, and *economic sociology*. In the widest sense, we recognize five major economic systems in the history of the Western world:

- Greek (Plato: 437–347 BCE; Aristotle: 384–322 BCE; Greece falls to the Romans in 146 BCE)
- Roman (Romulus, first king of Rome: 753–717 BCE; Augustus, first emperor, 27 BCE)
- Middle Ages (Feudalism): Fall of Rome (426) to Fall of Constantinople (1453)
- Mercantilism: fourteenth to early nineteenth century
- Liberalism/capitalism: from the Industrial Revolution (early nineteenth century) on – during this phase, political economy became a self-standing discipline.

Karl Marx (1818–83), the famous German philosopher and political economist, offered one of the most path-breaking analyses of the historical evolution of societies and their economic systems, embedded in what he called the process of *dialectical, historical materialism*. According to Marx, the western world moved from the agricultural system (which includes the stages of "primitive communism" and "slave societies") to feudalism to the current stage of capitalism; capitalism would then transition to socialism (workers also own the economy's capital) to then reach communism, the permanent and final social and economic system of his analysis, in which private property, and thus the class system, cease to exist.

Economic systems are studied in *particular* and *general* terms, that is, we can analyze either the economic behaviors of individual economic agents, such as the producer, the consumer, the worker, and so on; or we can analyze the functioning of the economic system as a whole. These two different perspectives give rise to the two fundamental approaches of economic analysis that are covered in this book: *microeconomics*, that focuses on the economic behavior of individual economic agents (Chapters 2, 3, and 4); and *macroeconomics*, that studies economies taken as a whole (Chapters 5, 6 and 7). In the next section you will encounter two major figures in the evolution of economics, Adam Smith (1723–90) and John Maynard Keynes (1883–1946): while Adam

Smith is generally recognized as the founder of political economy, Keynes introduced macroeconomic analysis in the discipline.

 ## 1.4 Founders of modern economics: Adam Smith and John Maynard Keynes

This section will only briefly discuss two of the most prominent figures in the field of *modern* economics: Adam Smith and John Maynard Keynes. Adam Smith's publication of *An Inquiry into the Nature and Causes of the Wealth of Nations* (1776) is generally considered the starting point of modern economics; and John Maynard Keynes' publication of *The General Theory of Employment, Interest, and Money* (1936) is considered the very first macroeconomic treatise.

Adam Smith

Adam Smith (b. Kirkaldy, 1723; d. Edinburgh, 1790), a moral philosopher by training and profession, published two books that marked the birth of economics as a self-standing discipline and provided the intellectual basis of what during the following century became known as capitalism: *The Theory of Moral Sentiments*, originally published in 1759 and which went through six editions during his life; and *An Inquiry into the Nature and Causes of the Wealth of Nations*, originally published in 1776 and which went through five editions in the course of his life. We will approach some of the most fundamental teachings of Adam Smith through an in-class exercise called Insight Dialogue. The text of the exercise is in the following two pages, and it will also be distributed in class.

■ ■ ■

Insight Dialogue 1

Instructions

All students need a partner in this exercise (the person on your right or on your left): connect for a moment with your partner. If you have not met your partner before, take a moment to introduce yourself. The instructor will take care of timekeeping, so there is no need for you to check your watch.

First 4 minutes: As the instructor signals the beginning of the exercise, immediately *start reading* the excerpts on the next page. Read carefully and swiftly, noticing what grabs your interest and makes you react the most. Feel free to underline, highlight, or make notations.

Next 2 minutes: At the instructor's signal, *stop reading*. Turn your attention inward and notice your personal reaction to what you read. What do you remember the most? Perhaps one excerpt had more effect on you than the others? Notice all that comes to mind … thoughts, emotions, memories. Stay with what comes up … do not worry about making your thoughts pretty, or acceptable!

Next 2 minutes: Again, at the instructor's signal, the first person of the pair talks continuously and expresses emotions, sensations, thoughts, memories, words triggered by the excerpts – without editing! The listener just witnesses/listens attentively: no speaking, nodding, making faces … whatsoever (it is NOT a conversation). Thus, it is not a matter of agreeing or not, or of sounding deep or educated or sophisticated; it is a matter of expressing whatever awareness the speaker has in the moment, and of being deeply listened to.

Next 2 minutes: At the signal, switch speakers.

Next 2 minutes: When the instructor signals the end of the "dialogue," go back to silence. Perhaps close your eyes, and notice what changed in your thinking or reaction to the excerpts after you spoke and after you listened …

– From Adam Smith (1759) *The Theory of Moral Sentiments*,
1st ed. (Part I, Section I, Chap. I; p. 1)

How selfish soever man may be supposed, there are evidently some principles in his nature, which interest him in the fortune of others, and render their happiness necessary to him, though he derives nothing from it except the pleasure of seeing it. Of this kind is pity or compassion, the emotion which we feel for the misery of others, when we either see it, or are made to conceive it in a lively manner. … Pity and compassion are words appropriated to signify our fellow-feeling with the sorrow of others. Sympathy … may be made use of to denote our fellow-feeling with any passion whatever.

– From Adam Smith (1976 [1776]) *An Inquiry into the Nature and Causes of the Wealth of Nations* (Book I, Chapter II; pp. 26–7)

But man has almost constant occasion for the help of his brethren, and it is in vain for him to expect it from their benevolence only. He will be more likely to prevail if he can interest their self-love in his favour, and shew them that it is for their own advantage to do for him what he requires of them. Whoever offers to another a bargain of any kind, proposes to do this. Give me that which I want, and you shall have this which you want, is the meaning of every such offer; and it is in this manner that we obtain from one another the far greater part of those good offices which we stand in need of. It is not from the benevolence of the butcher, the brewer, or the baker, that we expect our dinner, but from their regard to their own interest. We address ourselves, not to their humanity but to their self-love, and never talk to them of our own necessities but of their advantages.

– From Adam Smith (1976 [1790]) *The Theory of Moral Sentiments*, 6th ed. (Part I, Section III, Chap. III; pp. 61–2)

This disposition to admire, and almost to worship, the rich and the powerful, and to despise or, at least, to neglect, persons of poor and mean condition … is … the great and most universal cause of the corruption of our moral sentiments. That wealth and greatness are often regarded with the respect and admiration which are due only to wisdom and virtue; and that the contempt, of which vice and folly are the only proper objects, is most unjustly bestowed upon poverty and weakness, has been the complaint of moralists in all ages. We desire both to be respectable, and to be respected. We dread both to be contemptible, and to be contemned. But, upon coming into the world, we soon find that wisdom and virtue are by no means the sole objects of respect; nor vice and folly, of contempt. We frequently see the respectful attentions of the world more strongly directed towards the rich and the great, than towards the wise and the virtuous. We see frequently the vices and follies of the powerful much less despised than the poverty and weakness of the innocent. … Two different roads are presented to us, equally leading to the attainment of this so much desired object; the one, by the study of wisdom and the practice of virtue; the other, by the acquisition of wealth and greatness. Two different characters are presented to our emulation: the one, of proud ambition and ostentatious avidity; the other, of humble modesty and equitable justice.

■ ■ ■

How does this motivation of individual self-interest work for the economy? Adam Smith explains how self-interest and the economy relate to each other in the second chapter of Book IV of *The Wealth of Nations*:

As every individual … endeavors as much as he can both to employ his capital in the support of the domestic industry, and so to direct that industry that its produce may be of the greatest value; every individual necessarily labours to render the annual revenue of the society as great as he can. He generally, indeed, neither intends to promote the public interest, nor knows how much he is promoting it. By preferring the support of domestic to that of foreign industry, he intends only his own security; and by directing that industry in such a manner as its produce may be of the greatest value, he intends only his own gain, and he is in this, as in many other cases, led by *an invisible hand* to promote an end which was no part of his intention. Nor is it always the worse for the society that it was no part of it. **By pursuing his own interest he <u>frequently</u> promotes that of the society more effectively than when he really intends to promote it.** (p. 456)

The way one pursues "his own interest," in Adam Smith's vision of the human character, is instinctual, natural: it is through the *division of labor*, that is, specialization. Here is how he puts it in the first two chapters of *The Wealth of Nations*:

The greatest improvement in the productive powers of labour, and the greater part of the <u>skill, dexterity, and judgment</u> with which it is any where directed, or applied, seem to have been the effects of the division of labor. (p. 13)

This division of labour … is not originally the effect of any human wisdom, which foresees and intends that general opulence to which it gives occasion. It is the necessary, though very slow and gradual, consequence of a certain propensity in human nature which has in view no such extensive utility; the propensity to truck, barter, and exchange one thing for another. (p. 25)

According to Adam Smith, the way the wealth of a nation can be increased the most, where wealth is defined as the amount of "conveniences and necessities" its population can afford, is by letting individuals free to choose what and how to engage in the economy. This is the meaning of *laissez-faire*: <u>if there is an absolutely levelled playing field among the participants of the economy – we would say, in conditions of perfect competition</u> – then *laissez-faire* would indeed be the best option for the whole economy. Workers will find the occupations that pay the most given their talents, in the sectors where more investment has happened. And what are those sectors? They are those sectors in which the owners of capital (capitalists) obtain the highest profit. And why are those sectors providing the highest profits? Because the products of those sectors are the most desired by the consumers, who are therefore willing to pay a higher price. The same thing can be said about the owners of land, who will use the land in the way that provides the highest rent. It is a virtuous cycle that can only grow, at the ultimate satisfaction of the consumers, i.e., everybody.

Not only will the whole economy flourish, but everybody in the economy will benefit from it. This is the so-called underline{trickle down mechanism}, so that if a sector increases its production, it will send waves of demand to all the products and services that are necessary to the sector itself. It's a whole mechanism of markets linked one to the other, so that when the economy grows, it raises the standard of living of everybody in it. This economy can exist without regulation, without direction from above.

What role would then the government have? There are certain services that the government has to provide, services that nobody else has sufficient incentive to provide: justice, an army, infrastructure, and education. In addition, in Adam Smith's mind, the government has to be a watchdog, and make sure that nobody tries to stop or manipulate the "trickle down mechanism" and take advantage of her/his own power, and that the market functions freely and well (notice the word "frequently," purposely underlined, in the excerpt of the previous page). This of course was a major blow to the highly corrupted governments of the time, which completely controlled and greatly profited from the economy at the expense of the great majority of the population (think, for instance, of the "royal" East India Company, "royal" Dutch East India Company ...).

In conclusion, Adam Smith provided the blueprint of a *market economy*, of a *capitalist economy* (economic growth based on the accumulation of capital), and the specific conditions that would allow the so-called *laissez-faire* approach to economic policy to work well. The theoretical approach to the economy spurred by Adam Smith's contribution is known as *Classical* (and later *Neoclassical*) economics.

John Maynard Keynes

The most important and path-breaking work by Keynes is without doubt *The General Theory of Employment, Interest, and Money* (1936), the writing of which took place in the midst of the Great Depression, and which gave the very first fully fledged *macro*economic model to the discipline. From the beginning of the 1930s, Keynes had been especially concerned about the employment crisis, which was deepening drastically in the US and Great Britain. He made such concerns public many times: among them, an open letter to President Roosevelt published in *The New York Times* on December 31, 1933. In that letter, Keynes' path-breaking advice was to make vigorous use of fiscal policy (increase public spending and decrease taxation) to supplement the market mechanism of the private sector, which was clearly unable to correct the unemployment problem, and the advice was guardedly followed.

One of Keynes' most important theoretical contributions was his critique of Say's Law (an 1803 contribution by the French economist Jean Baptiste

Say, a.k.a. "supply creates demand," mentioned earlier and further discussed in Chapter 6), and in providing an alternative set of macroeconomic policies that would prove particularly useful in situations of recessions, that is, situations characterized by persistent, involuntary unemployment (where there are more people actively looking for jobs than available jobs). Say's Law fundamentally says that if the economy produces more goods, the economy will also *by itself* create the additional demand necessary to buy these goods. This seemingly innocuous idea, combined with the belief that markets work efficiently on their own, has an enormous theoretical consequence: that is, there cannot be persistent, involuntary unemployment in an economy! The rationale of this conclusion goes as follows: if there is involuntary unemployment, there will be workers who can't find a job and will be willing to work for a lower wage than the prevailing one. Wages therefore decrease, more workers are hired, and production of goods increases. The fact that more people are now at work has also increased people's income, and thus people's demand for goods. Thus, the additional goods produced find additional demand, while unemployment disappears.

This self-adjusting market mechanism failed to work during the Great Depression. Firms already had very high inventories, and even at lower wages did not want to hire more workers and produce more, because they did not trust that the additional output would be sold. A vicious cycle therefore began with increases in involuntary unemployment (firms firing people as they decreased production), decreases in people's incomes, decreases in people's demand for goods, and even higher unsold production for firms, that would decrease employment even more, and so on. Keynes offered a way to break this cycle, by showing that if the government intervened by directly creating more demand for goods and services and more income (by spending more and hiring more for public projects, providing more public subsidies), firms would see the demand for their goods increase, their inventories decrease, and would thus want to produce more, hire more, invest more, and so on. The vicious cycle would turn into a virtuous one.

We can stop here for now, as we will re-encounter Keynes later in the book: the Keynesian macroeconomic model will be the main macroeconomic theory you will be learning.

 ## 1.5 Alternative economic paradigms: feminist and ecological economics

As mentioned earlier, two important modern schools of economic thought are *feminist economics* and *ecological economics*. While feminism resurfaced in the US in the 1960s, it took until 1995 for the first (and still only)

journal dedicated to publishing the work of feminist economists to emerge. Feminist economists challenge several of the assumptions and tenets of both traditional and alternative economic theory, so the journey to establish the legitimacy of their ideas within the discipline has been on a long bumpy path that still encounters potholes and detours. Unlike Smithians and Keynesians, who each subscribe to a unique theoretical view, feminist economists represent a group of scholars who do not necessarily use the same paradigms or methodologies or the same theory. This group is unified by its understanding that gender, race, ethnicity, sexuality, and ability have been excised from economic theory and often policy. Feminist economists argue that this omission has resulted in economic paradigms that misconstrue an economy's structure and operation. Such omissions have often led to policies and outcomes that neglect or are deleterious to the lives of these groups. Feminist economists are unified in their desire to produce theoretical and analytical work that is inclusive in its representation of our society and the important roles played by these different social and economic groups.

One of the most important landmarks in feminist economics was the publication of Marianne Ferber and Julie Nelson's *Beyond Economic Man: Feminist Theory and Economics* in 1993. This edited book introduced many of the critiques of Neoclassical theory and its methodology that have come to be identified with feminist economists. Their follow-up book in 2003, *Feminist Economics Today: Beyond Economic Man*, provides a look at how these critiques have developed and the ideas as well as models that have been advanced to produce a more inclusive theoretical view.

Another important area of work of feminist economists is their critique of and proposals for measurements of economic activity. Marilyn Waring (1988) initiated this work after she spent years as a New Zealand representative in Parliament and came to understand how both developed and developing countries by relying on the traditional measures of economic activity made invisible the work that was not included within the usual sphere of the market: child and elder care; meal planning, preparation, and clean-up; house management, and many others. You will be introduced to measures of economic activity in later chapters, but the one on which she focused was the Gross Domestic Product (Chapter 5). Most of these economic measures rely on a market exchange to provide values for the various activities. Those activities that occur outside the market sphere have no value, so they are ignored. Waring and others who have followed in her footsteps have argued that in both developed and developing countries the omission of this work leads to an incomplete view of the economy's activity and the important actors in it. They have proposed and, in many cases, have succeeded in having governments adopt expanded or additional measurements that capture these key economic actors and activities.

Ecological economists have noted that Neoclassical theory ignores another important area for the economy: the contributions of nature. In 1982, the first symposium on "Integrating Ecology and Economics," was held in Stockholm, Sweden, organized by Ann-Mari Jansson, an ecologist who would play a key role in the establishment of the new field. Further meetings followed this, and, in 1989, the first issue of the academic journal *Ecological Economics* was published. Ecological economists such as Robert Costanza and Herman Daly argued that Neoclassical economics glossed over the important fact that all material products that are transformed by production in the economic system come from nature, and they eventually return to nature as waste. Such natural resources (or natural capital) cannot be completely replaced by human-produced products without upsetting a careful balance (Costanza, Daly, and Bartholomew, 1991). That is, there are complex interactions between the economic and environmental systems, and the growth of the economic system can ultimately interfere with the functioning of the environment, as we see most starkly with the issue of anthropogenic (human-caused) climate change.

While many economists studying the environment using the Neoclassical approach believe that these issues can be solved simply by properly valuing and pricing environmental resources, services, and wastes (discussed in Chapter 3), ecological economists go further. They argue that because resources are finite and the ability of the environment to absorb waste is finite, the growth of material production must be carefully controlled. However, the evolution of the economic system (the sorts of things that are produced, whom they are produced for, and how production is organized) can continue. As a result, economists should more carefully consider the goals of economic growth: how can well-being be most enhanced for the most people using the fewest possible resources?

You'll read more about work in feminist and ecological economics in Chapter 8.

Note

1. The distinction between *economics* and *political economy* became meaningful only at the turn of the twentieth century, with the publication of the very first *Principles of Economics* by the British economist Alfred Marshall, in 1890. Until then all textbooks of *economics* were in fact entitled *Principles of Political Economy*, and all scholars in the field self-identified as "political economists".

References

Aristotle (350 BCE) *Politics*, translated by Benjamin Howett, *The Internet Classics Archive*. http://classics.mit.edu/Aristotle/politics.html.

Bacon, Francis (2000 [1620–26]) *The Instauratio Magna: Last Writings*, The Oxford Francis Bacon, Vol. XIII. Oxford: Clarendon Press.

Costanza, Robert, Daly, Herman E., and Bartholomew, Joy A. (ed.) (1991) "Goals, Agenda, and Policy Recommendations for Ecological Economics," in *Ecological Economics: The Science and Management of Sustainability*. New York: Columbia University Press.

Ferber, Marianne A. and Nelson, Julie A. (eds.) (1993) *Beyond Economic Man: Feminist Theory and Economics*. Chicago: University of Chicago Press.

Ferber, Marianne A. and Nelson, Julie A. (eds.) (2003) *Feminist Economics Today: Beyond Economic Man*. Chicago: University of Chicago Press.

Keynes, John Maynard (1936) *The General Theory of Employment, Interest, and Money*. London: Macmillan.

Mill, John S. (1848) *Principles of Political Economy*. Reprint. Fairfield NJ: Augustus M. Kelley Publishers.

Robbins, Lionel (1932) *An Essay on the Nature and Significance of Economic Science*. London: MacMillan & Co.

Robinson, Joan. (1970) *Freedom and Necessity*. London: George Allen & Unwin Ltd.

Sismondi, Sismonde de (1847 [1834]) "On the Conditions of the Work People in Manufactories," in *Political Economy and the Philosophy of Government*. London: John Chapman, pp. 196–223.

Smith, Adam (1759) *The Theory of Moral Sentiments*. 1st ed. London: A. Millar.

Smith, Adam (1976 [1790]) *The Theory of Moral Sentiments*. 6th ed. Oxford: Oxford University Press.

Smith, Adam (1976 [1776]) *An Inquiry into the Nature and Causes of the Wealth of Nations*. Oxford: Oxford University Press.

Waring, Marilyn (1988) *If Women Counted: A New Feminist Economics*. San Francisco: Harper & Row.

2

Not in the Garden of Eden

Scarcity and tradeoffs

 ## 2.1 Scarcity and inevitable trade-off among activities

Karl Marx described *society* as a *system meant to satisfy human needs and wants on the basis of means and rules.*[1] This seems a very simple way of thinking about society, but in fact it contains a realization that sets us up for a great introduction to economic analysis. This realization consists of the fact that while human wants are infinite, the means to satisfy them, that is, the resources available, are finite. This points us directly to the *realm* of economics, which is a world of *scarcity*. If the essential resources that need to be used to satisfy all human needs and wants are scarce (which means that they are in limited, finite supply), then what logic do we follow in order to allocate them across various uses? If we allocate more of a finite resource to a particular use, we will necessarily have to allocate less of that finite resource to other uses: the concept of scarcity goes hand-in-hand with the idea of trade-off among alternative uses. Thus, the title of this chapter: *not in the Garden of Eden*. We need to make choices; we need to choose how finite resources could/ should be allocated among alternative uses, with the understanding that if we allocate more to a specific use, we will have to allocate less to something else. In other words, we need to choose how different uses of given, finite resources may be or may not be prioritized.

We can think of this problem at our own individual level: we use economics every time we have a finite resource, such as money or time, and we consider alternative uses of that finite resource for activities we do care about. This problem appears all the time also at a social, collective level: for instance, how does Congress establish government spending priorities?

■ ■ ■

Opportunity for further reflection/discussion: Are human wants and needs indeed unlimited? What determines wants and needs? What does *greed* have to do with this? Is greed innate? If wants were not unlimited, would *scarcity* still matter?

■ ■ ■

The way in which this problem of choice is analyzed depends on whether we are looking at the tree or the whole forest, that is, whether we are only concerned about allocating a finite resource to *one* specific use independently of anything else, or whether we are concerned about all the alternative uses of the finite resource. Let's begin from the simplest scenario: suppose first that our concern is whether we should use some finite resource for *one particular use*: for instance, should we use some wood logs to build a cabin? This seems a pretty trivial inquiry, but even this has its layer of complications. First of all, we need to realize that, if an essential resource is scarce (finite), then it's not free: it must have a <u>cost</u> (if the resource is *essential* to obtaining something desirable, then there will be some degree of competition for its use, giving to the owners of the resource the opportunity to charge a price for it). And if we are willing to use a costly resource for a particular activity, it must be that someone gives value to that activity. That is, the activity must yield some <u>*benefit*</u> (to someone). Then, our first economic problem becomes: <u>should this activity be performed?</u> Well …

If   Benefits > Costs   DO IT

If   Benefits < Costs   DON'T DO IT

If   Benefits = Costs   IT DOESN'T MATTER WHETHER YOU DO IT OR NOT!

This is known as a <u>*cost-benefit analysis*</u>: once all benefits and costs associated with the activity are identified, the analysis fundamentally becomes the comparison of two "numbers." And now, the real bulk of complications: the identification of costs and benefits is most of the time difficult, as there are costs and benefits that do not have a market value, and thus are not readily quantifiable. For instance, think about the decision to utilize some land for a public park. The cost might be easily quantifiable, but what about the benefit? Or think about the decision of building a nuclear power plant: the benefits might be easily measurable, but what about the costs? The cost of a book you are thinking of buying (thus allocating some of your finite budget to it) is easily determined, but what about the quantification of the benefit of buying the book? Have you ever felt uncertain about whether to buy something or not because you were not sure whether "it was worth it"? How do you figure out what to do, in those circumstances?

More interesting is the case in which we care about the whole forest, that is, we care to choose the allocation of a finite resource across all its competing, alternative uses. Here, the cost of allocating the finite resource to one use is the inevitable reduction in other possible uses. For simplicity, let's imagine that the whole forest consists of just two trees (overall, only two possible uses for the same, finite resource). Then, when the resource is fully used (no slack), if we wish to obtain more of one use, we necessarily will be able to obtain less of the other. This is where the problem of choice becomes really apparent, and more cumbersome. This problem of choice leads us to the next two economic concepts.

2.2 Production Possibility Frontier (PPF) and opportunity cost

Imagine that your local City Council is figuring out how to spend a given amount of public funds between *city infrastructure* (for instance, improvement of sidewalks and city streets) and *building public housing* (notice that this is the same as saying that the City Council is about to decide how to allocate a finite resource between two alternative uses: infrastructure and public housing). In order for a decision to be made, the City Council will first need to know what sort of alternative combinations of infrastructure and public housing can be achieved given the finite amount of available funds, and thus given the finite resources that can be bought with those funds.

A graph, Figure 2.1, greatly simplifies this task: set up a Cartesian map that measures the two alternative uses (*infrastructure* and *housing*) on the axes. Assume that a given amount of resources is available and fully and efficiently utilized in the production of the two categories of goods. Consider also the possibility that some resources may be better utilized in one use, some in the other (yet all resources can be, and are, used). Let's also assume that we do this analysis at a given moment in time, so that the technology used in production is set and constant, it cannot change in that moment. Begin with the idea that all resources are allocated to one of the two uses. Then imagine we increase the other use: the most appropriate resources to the second use will be the first ones to switch (for instance, if we have infrastructure on the vertical axis, civil engineers, land, etc. will switch first). This will give a big boost to the second use without sacrificing a lot of the first (as we are assuming that the first resources that switch from infrastructure to building are more appropriate for the construction of buildings than for the improvement of infrastructure). Then, imagine we continue with this process, and keep switching to public housing resources that are more and more appropriate for the improvement of infrastructure, and less and less appropriate for the construction of public housing (perhaps, the last resource that switches uses is … asphalt). We keep going until we reach the other axis.

We obtain a negatively sloped curve, that shows all the possibilities of production of the two alternative uses, given the resources available and technology in use. We call this curve the *Production Possibility Frontier* (or Curve), often simply indicated as "PPF".

FIGURE 2.1   Production Possibility Frontier (PPF)

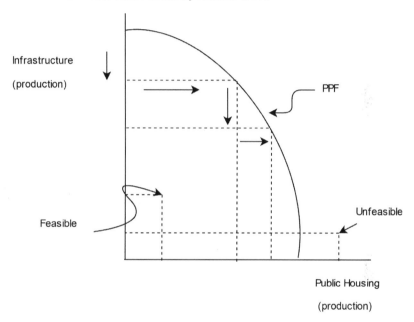

When we look at the PPF described in Figure 2.1, we can see that there are three different positions in the figure. The combinations of goods and services that are "inside" the PPF are feasible (given the amount of resources and the technology available); the combinations of goods and services that are "outside" the PPF are unfeasible; and, finally, the combinations of goods and services that are exactly on the PPF efficiently exhaust all the resources available (full-employment of the available resources).

General definition of Production Possibility Frontier: set of all the combinations of goods and services that can be obtained given the full employment of the finite resources and the efficient use of technology.

Inherent to the frontier is the quantification of the trade-offs between one use and the other. This *quantification of the trade-off* is also a very important concept in economics: it is the concept of opportunity cost.

But before we get there, let's just think for a moment about what determines, and thus might change, the position and shape of the PPF:

1. What happens if resources become more abundant? There's an expansion of the PPF, possibly biased towards one of the two uses depending on how specialized the utilization of resources is.
2. What happens if technology improves? The same finite resources can now produce more: again, expansion of the PPF, possibly biased towards one of the two uses depending on the characteristics of the technological improvement.

■ ■ ■

Opportunity for further reflection: what would the PPF look like if resources were not specialized and could be moved easily and without any loss of efficiency from one use to the other?

■ ■ ■

Back now to the quantification of the trade-off mentioned earlier, i.e., to the concept of *opportunity cost*. It's a very familiar, intuitive, and … tricky concept to learn, so let's start with a complete definition of it.

General definition of opportunity cost: Given two activities (A and B) that use at least one common and finite resource, there must be a trade-off between them: the more activity A is performed, the less activity B can be performed. The opportunity cost of A in terms of B is the reduction suffered by activity B in order to obtain one additional unit of activity A. Notice that the opportunity cost can only be positive.

EXAMPLES

1. Johnnie dedicates 12 hours a month to cleaning his apartment (Activity A: "C" as in "Cleaning") and to doing laundry (Activity B: "L" as in "Load of Laundry"). It takes him an average of 3 hours to clean his place, and about 1 hour and a half to do a load of laundry. Let's draw Johnnie's PPF, find the equation of the PPF, and determine the opportunity cost of cleaning the apartment in terms of loads of laundry.

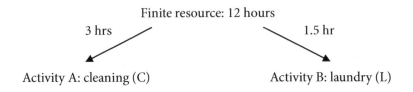

Finite resource: 12 hours

3 hrs   1.5 hr

Activity A: cleaning (C)   Activity B: laundry (L)

To draw the PPF: set up your Cartesian map; label axes with C and L (notice that on the axes we have the alternative uses of the finite resource, NOT the finite resource itself, which remains implicit/hidden in the graph).

Max number of C, when Johnnie does zero loads of laundry: 12/3 = 4
Max number of L, when Johnnie never cleans the apartment: 12/1.5 = 8

FIGURE 2.2   Johnnie's Production Possibility Frontier

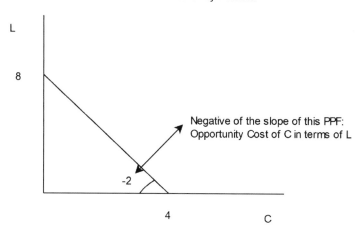

EQUATION OF THE PPF:

$(3\,hrs) * C + (1.5\,hrs) * L = 12\,hrs$ [the PPF implies full-employment of the given resource]

$3C + 1.5L = 12$
$1.5L = -3C + 12$
$L = -2C + 8$ [Johnnie's PPF, expressed with L on the vertical axis]

Slope of PPF: – "rise"/"run" = – 8/4 = – 2

Opportunity cost of C in terms of L, that is, how many L does Johnnie have to forego in order to do one more apartment cleaning C? It takes 3 hours to clean the apartment; how many loads of laundry can he do in 3 hours? 2 loads of L. Thus, the opportunity cost of C in terms of L is: 2 loads of L.

Notice that the opportunity cost of C in terms of L is *the negative of the slope of the PPF, when C is on the horizontal axis*, which leads us to the following general rule: the negative of the slope of the PPF is the opportunity cost of the activity on the horizontal axis in terms of the activity on the vertical axis. This is always true.

2.   Suppose that one acre of land can produce either 2,000 pounds of wheat (W) or 10,000 pounds of strawberries (S). Suppose that this land can be

utilized for one or the other use without loss of efficiency. Draw the PPF (with W on the vertical axis) and determine the opportunity cost of 1 pound of wheat in terms of pounds of strawberries.

The PPF, Figure 2.3, is easy to draw, as we already have the intercepts of the PPF with the axes (the maximum amount of S when no W is produced; and the maximum amount of W when no S is produced).

FIGURE 2.3   Production Possibility Frontier: Strawberries & Wheat

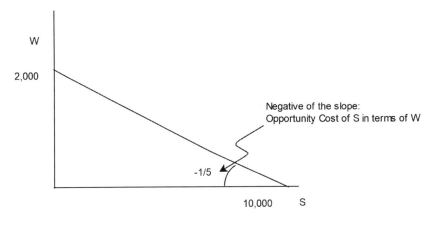

Slope of PPF = − 2.000/10,000 = −1/5

OC of S in terms of W: you would have to forego 1/5 of a pound of W to produce one additional pound of S.

The question, however, asks you to find the OC of W in terms of S, that is, how many pounds of S you would have to forego to produce one more pound of W. Let's be more specific with our reasoning then.

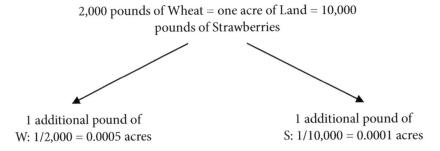

2,000 pounds of Wheat = one acre of Land = 10,000 pounds of Strawberries

1 additional pound of
W: 1/2,000 = 0.0005 acres

1 additional pound of
S: 1/10,000 = 0.0001 acres

In order to produce one more pound of W, 0.0005 acres would have to be withdrawn from the production of S and allocated to the production of W. How many pounds of S would 0.0005 acres of land produce? Given that it takes 0.0001 acre to produce 1 pound of S, if we withdraw 0.0005 acres of land from the production of S we forego the production of (.0005/.0001) = 5 pounds of S. Thus, the OC of W in terms of S is: 5 (pounds of S).

Notice that:

OC of S in terms of W: 1/5 (pounds of W)
OC of W in terms of S: 5 (pounds of S)

This leads us to another <u>general rule</u> for opportunity costs: <u>if the opportunity cost of A in terms of B is X, the opportunity cost of B in terms of A is 1/X.</u>

▓ 2.3 A special case of PPF: the budget constraint

The Production Possibility Frontier tells us which outcomes are feasible and which are unfeasible given two alternative uses of a finite resource, the technology in use (or how much finite resource is necessary to obtain one unit of each alternative use), and the amount of finite resource available. We can easily apply this way of analyzing the effects of scarcity on choice from the realm of production to the realm of consumption.

If we translate the concept of production possibility frontier to our own lives, it seems that we often find ourselves in situations in which, willingly or not, we deal with a particular specification of PPF: How many times have you gone to a store with a <u>given budget</u> and tried to "allocate" this budget onto alternative uses?

When we consider "a budget" as our "finite resource," and the "prices" of the alternative uses as the unitary amounts of finite resource necessary to obtain one unit of each alternative "use," we obtain a "budget-related" PPF that results from applying exactly the same procedure learned earlier. This particular PPF goes under the name of <u>budget constraint.</u>

<u>General definition of budget constraint</u>: the budget constraint is the possibility frontier that indicates all the combination of goods and services that can be purchased given a finite amount of income (budget) and given the prices of these goods and services.

The combinations of goods and services that are "inside" the budget constraint are <u>affordable</u>; the combinations of goods and services that are "outside" the budget constraint are <u>not affordable</u>; and finally, the combinations of goods and services that are exactly on the budget constraint exhaust all the budget available.

Assume that we have TWO alternative uses of our budget. What would a budget constraint look like? The process is completely analogous to that seen in the case of a PPF, and can be best appreciated with an example.

Suppose we have a weekly budget of $200, and that the alternative uses of this budget are: sodas (S), at a unitary price of $2, and veggie-burgers (V), at a unitary price of $4. Let's draw our budget constraint and find the corresponding equation.

- The maximum number of sodas we can buy – if we don't buy any veggie-burgers – is: 100 sodas.
- The maximum number of veggie-burgers we can buy – if we don't buy any soda – is: 50 burgers.

Then, prepare a diagram with, say, veggie-burgers on the vertical axis and sodas on the horizontal axis. Draw the line that connects the max affordable number of burgers (when sodas are "zero", and the max affordable number of sodas (when burgers are "zero"). That's your budget constraint. Make sure you can interpret it.

FIGURE 2.4   Budget constraint: veggie-burgers and sodas

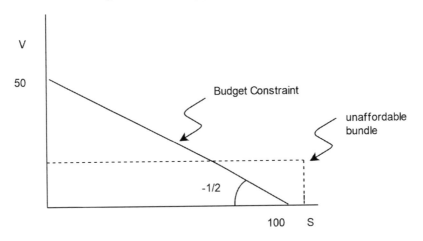

Budget constraint equation

$2 \times S + $4 \times V = 200

$4V = -2S + 200$ [given that V is on the vertical axis]

$V = -\frac{1}{2}S + 50$ equation representing the budget constraint [with V on the vertical axis]

■ ■ ■

Opportunities for further reflection

1. How do you interpret the slope of the budget constraint in terms of opportunity cost? Opportunity cost of what in terms of what? What does the number you obtain mean in practical terms?
2. What would change the position of this budget constraint?
3. Why is the budget constraint a "line" and not a "curve"?

■ ■ ■

Note

1. You may want to notice how similar this statement is to Lionel Robbins' definition of *economy* encountered in the previous chapter: What's the difference between the two? How important would you say this difference might be?

3

Led by an invisible hand

The market

▌ 3.1 Markets: a general introduction

We are now ready to introduce one of the most important conceptual frameworks in the study of microeconomics: the concept of the "market."

Definition of market: the geographical or conceptual space dedicated to the interactions between economic agents (individuals, firms, and the government) who want to buy a good/service and economic agents who want to sell that particular good/service. Economic agents who want to buy a good/service are said to express a demand for that good/ service. Economic agents who want to sell a good/service are said to express a supply for that good/service. An outcome of the interactions between buyers and sellers of a good/service is the determination of its market price.

The function of a market – and the way a market works – can be easily understood if you think of the actual function of street markets. If you happen to visit the bazaar of Istanbul or the *souk* of Marrakesh, for instance, you will inevitably notice that sellers keep calling prices for what they have to sell, and buyers keep negotiating for better prices. Sellers want to obtain the highest possible price, and buyers want to pay as little as possible. At some point the sale is done, at a price that is a compromise between the higher prices asked by the seller and the lower prices offered by the buyer. In the bazaar or the *souk* this is all typically done loudly and in the open, not something we see very often, but it is a great example of how all markets actually work, even though they do this less visibly.

The function of the market is to make transactions possible, by determining a price at which buyers and sellers are willing to buy and sell the same amount of the good or service in question. Another way to say this is that, in general, a market for a good or service identifies the *equilibrium price* at which the quantity of that specific good/service demanded by consumers *becomes* equal to the quantity supplied by sellers. This equilibrium price, of course, depends on the relative strength of the demand and the supply of the good/service. Typically, the relative strength of demand and supply, and thus the corresponding equilibrium price, keep changing through time.

An example of the dynamic nature of equilibrium prices, perhaps familiar to those who happen to get news updates during the business hours of the New York Stock Exchange, is given by the large number of stock prices which tend to change many times per minute. A simpler, slower, and more detailed example of the dynamic nature of an equilibrium price in response to changes in demand and supply is provided by the shifts undergone by the U.S. market of corn about 10 years ago (data from the USDA's National Agriculture Statistical Service[1]):

- in 2005 the price of corn in the US market was $2.60/bushel;
- during 2005, high oil prices and instability in the Middle East produced incentives to get corn-based ethanol as a fuel substitute for gasoline; new ethanol plants began purchasing more corn. The demand for corn increased, creating a <u>shortage</u> (larger quantity demanded than supplied) of corn. Consumers of corn began to bid against each other to obtain corn, making the price of corn increase. Observing the rising prices of corn, suppliers of corn saw the opportunity of increasing their profits by producing more corn, thus allowing the supply of corn to meet the increased demand;
- by 2007, the US market for corn reached a first peak of $5.12/bushel; the price of corn continued to rise, reaching $7.51/bushel by 2012 (an increase of 188% since 2005!)

In order to be able to study these market dynamics, we need to characterize a market in a more analytical way. Let's study the most important determinants of market demand and market supply separately first, and then allow them to interact in the space we have called *market*.

■ ■ ■

Opportunity for further reflection/discussion

Can you think of other types of arrangements, institutions, besides markets, that allow for the satisfaction of needs/wants by consumers, and for the distribution of goods/services by suppliers? Have markets always existed? What do you think the incentive(s) for consumers and for producers to participate in *markets* might be?

■ ■ ■

▓ 3.2 Market demand

Let's start our discussion of the determinants of the market demand of a good/service with an example that may be very familiar to all of us: the market demand for smartphones. As we begin to think about the determinants of the quantity demanded of smartphones at any given time (that is, what may affect consumers' decisions to buy more or fewer smartphones), we may come up with a long list of potential factors, such as:

- The price of smartphones
- The price of other related goods (cellular contracts, other phones, tablets, etc.)
- Tastes and preferences (including the effects of marketing)
- Consumers' income
- Expectations of the future price of smartphones
- The number of consumers
- Other factors (availability and quality of cellular networks, and so on …)

How do we rationalize the impact of so many factors on the quantity demanded of smartphones, so that we can make some sense of under what circumstances the quantity demanded of a good may increase or decrease?

The first thing we can do is to only keep those factors listed above that we think may have the *strongest* impact on the quantity demanded of smartphones. There is general agreement that the most important determinants of the market quantity demanded of any good/service are:

- The price of the good/service
- The prices of related goods/services
- The income of consumers
- Tastes/preferences of consumers
- The number of consumers

But even with this simplification, we still have at least five variables at play (actually many more, depending on the number of related goods/services!), which would make it impossible for us to even have a graphical representation of their impact on the quantity demanded of a good. How can this problem be simplified further?

Economics uses again and again a very helpful strategy to get around this problem of high dimensionality, that is, of more than three variables interacting at the same time: the assumption of *ceteris paribus*, which literally means "all other things constant." Of all the variables the market quantity demanded of smartphones depends on, we keep every variable except the price of smartphones constant (for the moment) and just study the specific relationship between market quantity demanded and price of smartphones. We say: *given* the consumers' tastes, income, and price of other goods (say, the average price of cellular service and the average price of tablets), how does the market quantity demanded of smartphones change in relation to the price of smartphones? Given that everything else remains constant during the course of this experiment, it is quite intuitive to imagine that the higher the price of *smartphones* is, the fewer of them will be bought by consumers.

Thus, *given income, tastes, and prices of other goods, there is an inverse relationship between the quantity demanded of a good and the price of the good*: this is known as the <u>LAW OF DEMAND</u>.

Notice that by convention the demand curve (always a line in this book, but not in real life) is <u>always</u> drawn with the *price of the good* on the vertical axis and the *quantity demanded of the good* on the horizontal axis, even though in our construction it is the *quantity demanded* that is a function of the *price*, and so from a mathematical point of view, *quantity demanded*, as the dependent variable, should be on the vertical axis, and *price*, as the independent variable, should be on the horizontal axis, as in Figure 3.1. That's not the way we draw it, though!

FIGURE 3.1   Graphical representation of a generic market demand

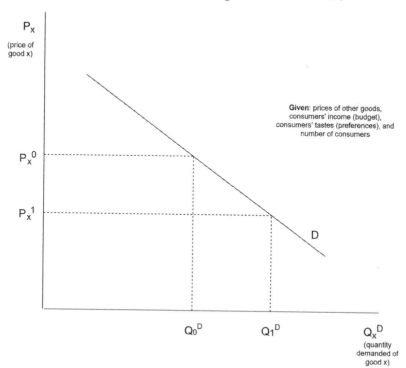

Working with the *ceteris paribus* assumption

The market demand for smartphones has been drawn while keeping the price of cell contracts, the price of tablets (in general we would say: the prices of all other goods), consumers' tastes, consumers' income, and number of consumers all constant. What happens when one of these variable changes? In order to see this, we apply the same *ceteris paribus* strategy used above: as we conduct each experiment, we imagine all variables constant except the one we are specifically concerned with.

<u>Tastes</u>: this is the simplest change. If consumers happen to develop a taste (that is, it becomes more fashionable or desirable) for smartphones, the quantity of smartphones they will want to buy <u>at any given price</u> will tend to increase. Graphically, the whole demand shifts to the right if consumers develop a taste for smartphones (and to the left if consumers develop a dislike for smartphones). To see this, assume any given price (and every other variable except tastes) remains fixed for a moment, and, then, ask yourself the question: if consumers develop a taste for this good, what will happen to the quantity demanded? It will increase, and thus the demand will have to shift to the right, as in Figure 3.2.

FIGURE 3.2   Effect of an increase in the desire for a good (generic)

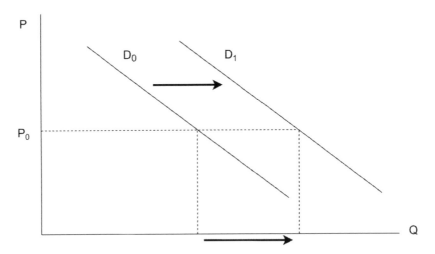

Income: if consumers' income increases, it is very likely that they will want to buy a higher quantity of smartphones, at any given price of smartphones. Goods for which an increase in income leads to an increase in the quantity demanded (*ceteris paribus*) are called <u>normal goods</u>: for these goods, when income increases the demand curve shifts to the right, as in Figure 3.3. Most goods are normal goods.

FIGURE 3.3   Effect of an increase in income: normal goods (generic)

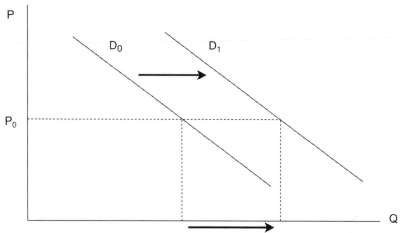

There is however a category of goods for which an increase in income tends to be associated with a decrease in the quantity demanded (*ceteris paribus*). A favorite example of these goods seems to be Top Ramen! These are goods that are purchased only at relatively low levels of income: as income increases, consumers tend to move to better quality goods. These goods are called <u>inferior goods</u>. For these goods, when income increases the demand curve shifts to the left, as in Figure 3.4.

FIGURE 3.4   Effect of an increase in income: inferior goods (generic)

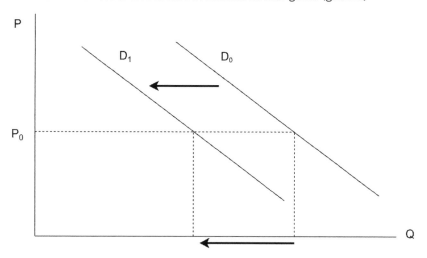

<u>Note</u>: The case of a decrease in income implies symmetrical, opposite shifts.

Prices of other goods: when the price of other goods increases (*ceteris paribus*) the quantity demanded of smartphones may increase or decrease depending on whether the "other goods" are perceived as *substitutes* or *complements* of smartphones. For instance, if the price of cellular service increases, it seems reasonable to think that the quantity of smartphones people may want to buy at any given smartphone price will tend to decrease, as the "whole package" of using a smartphone has become more expensive. We say that smartphones and cellular service contracts are perceived as *complements*: when the price of a complement increases (*ceteris paribus*), the demand shifts to the left, as seen in Figure 3.5.

If, instead, the price of tablets increases (*ceteris paribus*), and if we assume that consumers generally perceive tablets and smartphones as *substitutes* (they satisfy many of the same needs), then it is likely that fewer people will buy tablets and more people will buy smartphones (as smartphones have become relatively cheaper than tablets now). In this case, we say that smartphones and tablets are perceived as *substitutes*: when the price of a substitute increases (*ceteris paribus*), the demand shifts to the right, as in Figure 3.6.

FIGURE 3.5   Effect of an increase in the price of a complement of good X on the demand for good X

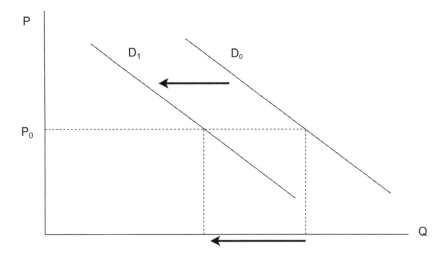

FIGURE 3.6   Effect of an Increase in the price of a substitute of good X on the demand for good X

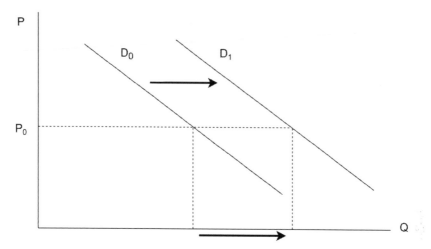

Note: The case of a decrease in the price of a complement/substitute implies symmetrical, opposite shifts.

■ ■ ■

Practice exercise

Globalization changes the number of consumers of most goods. In the case of American smartphones, globalization increases the number of consumers. Draw a generic market demand for smartphones and show the effect on the demand of an increase in the number of consumers.

■ ■ ■

Finally, let's have an <u>algebraic formulation of the market demand</u> (a.k.a. demand function, or demand schedule, or demand curve: all synonyms). Any line or curve that shows a negative relationship between price and quantity of a good, *ceteris paribus*, can be interpreted as a market demand. The simplest possible formulation may be something like:

$$P = b - aQ \tag{3.1}$$

Where:

- "a" and "b" are positive numbers,
- "P" indicates the price of a good,
- "– a" is the slope of the line,
- "Q" indicates the quantity demanded of the good,
- "b" is the intercept of the line with the vertical axis, which tells us the price at which the quantity demanded of the good becomes zero.

FIGURE 3.7 Graph of the demand function: $P = b - aQ$

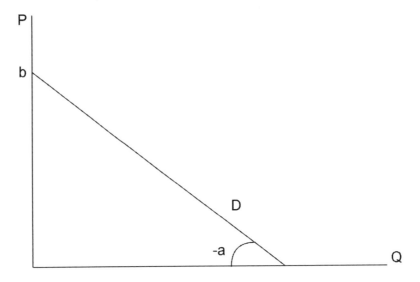

EXAMPLE

Draw the following demand function: $P = 100 - 0.5Q$.

To draw this function:

- intercept with vertical axis: 100
- intercept with horizontal axis, i.e., value of Q when P = 0: Q = 200
- draw the line that connects the two points: that's the market demand.

FIGURE 3.8   Graph of the demand function: $P = 100 - 0.5Q$

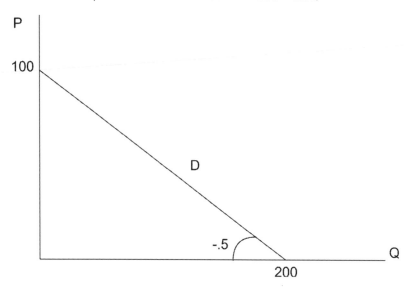

3.3 Market supply

A similar conceptual process will guide us in identifying the market supply of smartphones. Put yourself in the shoes of a producer of smartphones: what would make you produce a higher quantity of them? Whatever may increase the producers' profits will make them produce more of the good. Profits are defined as *revenues* obtained from the sale of the good produced, minus the production *costs* incurred by the firm. So: <u>whatever increases revenues or decreases costs of producing smartphones will make producers produce more smartphones</u>. A list of factors that affect the market supply of smartphones includes:

- The price of smartphones
- Costs of resources and factors of production/inputs, such as labor, parts, etc.
- Technology (how much of each input is necessary to produce one unit of output)
- The number of suppliers

Again, let's prioritize the relationship between price of the good and quantity supplied (produced) of the good, while keeping all other determinants of the market quantity supplied constant (we are applying again the *ceteris paribus* assumption). Again, we ask the question: <u>given</u> the cost of inputs, technology, and number of firms producing the good, how does the market quantity supplied of smartphones change in relation to the price of smartphones? Given

that everything else remains constant during the course of this thought experiment, it is quite intuitive to imagine that the higher the price of smartphones
is, the more of them will be supplied by the producers. See Figure 3.9.

   Thus, *given cost of inputs, technology, and number of suppliers, there is a
positive relationship between the market quantity supplied of a good and the
price of the good*: this is known as the LAW OF SUPPLY.

FIGURE 3.9   Generic graphical representation of the market supply

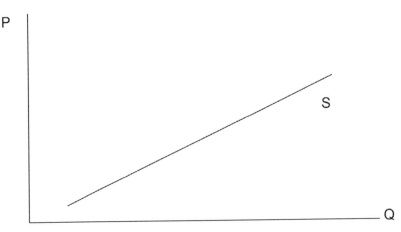

Notice that by convention the supply is also <u>always</u> drawn with the price of the
good on the vertical axis and the quantity of the good on the horizontal axis.

■ ■ ■

Practice exercise

The above market supply has been drawn while keeping the cost of
inputs, technology, and the number of suppliers all constant. How would
you shift the supply when:

- the cost of inputs (such as the average wage) increases, *ceteris
  paribus*?
- there is some technology improvement in the production of the
  good, *ceteris paribus*?

■ ■ ■

And, finally, as we did for the demand, let's have an <u>algebraic formulation
of the market supply</u> (a.k.a. supply function, or supply schedule, or supply

curve: all synonyms). Any line or curve that shows a positive relationship between price and quantity of a good, *ceteris paribus*, can be interpreted as a market supply. The simplest possible formulation may be something like:

$$P = cQ + d \qquad\qquad (3.2)$$

Where:

- "c" and "d" are positive numbers,
- "P" indicates the price of a good,
- "c" is the (positive) slope of the line,
- "Q" indicates the market quantity supplied of the good,
- "d" is the intercept of the line with the vertical axis, which tells us the price at which the quantity supplied of the good becomes zero.

FIGURE 3.10 Graph of the supply function: $P = cQ + d$

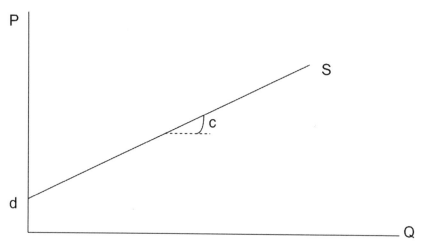

EXAMPLE

Given the following supply function: $P = Q + 10$, draw the corresponding graph.

To draw this supply:

- intercept with vertical axis: 10
- find a second point of the supply: give "Q" any value and find the corresponding "P". For instance: if $Q = 20$, then $P = 30$.
- draw the line that connects the two points: that's the market supply.

FIGURE 3.11   Graphical representation of the supply function: $P = Q + 10$

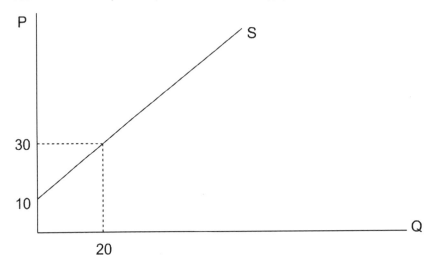

3.4 Price adjustment mechanism (market mechanism)

We can now allow both consumers and suppliers of smartphones – or any good or service for which there is a demand and supply – to interact with each other in the marketplace. Consumers' behavior is fully described by their market demand; producers' behavior is fully described by the market supply; and the marketplace is described as the "overlap" of market demand and supply of the good (consumers and suppliers occupy the same conceptual – or geographical – space: the *market*), as shown in Figure 3.12.

Let's see how consumers and suppliers may interact with each other. In Figure 3.12, suppose that for some reason the initial price of the good is P_0. Then, consumers will want to buy Q_0^D units of the good, and producers will bring to the market Q_0^S units of the good (read consumers' behavior on the demand function, and producers' behavior on the supply function). There will be an <u>excess demand, or shortage</u>, in this market, as at P_0 consumers want to buy more units than there are on the market. Consumers will begin to outbid each other in order to obtain the good (think about the housing market during a boom, for instance): the price of the good will begin to increase! As the price increases, consumers will begin to decrease the number of units they want to buy, while producers will want to supply a higher number of units. The tendency for the price to increase will continue as long as there is a shortage of the good: it will stop *only* when the price has reached the value P*, the *equilibrium price*, at which the quantity demanded

FIGURE 3.12   The market

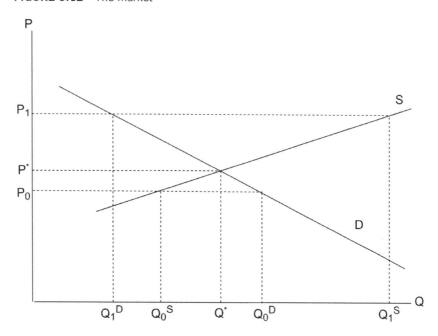

of the good is equal to the quantity supplied of the good: Q*. Only at P* there is no more pressure for the price of the good to further change: the market is in *equilibrium*.

Again, in Figure 3.12, suppose instead that for some reason the initial price of the good is P_1. Then, consumers will want to buy Q_1^D units of the good, and producers will bring to the market Q_1^S units of the good. There will be an <u>excess supply, or surplus</u>, in this market, as at P_1 consumers want to buy fewer units than there are on the market. Suppliers will begin to outbid each other in order to sell the units of goods available at their stores (think about the buy-one-get-one-free sales at department stores, for instance): the price of the good will begin to decrease! As the price decreases, consumers will increase the number of units they want to buy, while producers will begin to supply fewer units. The tendency for the price to decrease will continue as long as there is a surplus of the good: it will stop *only* once the price has reached the value P*, the *equilibrium price*, at which the quantity demanded of the good is equal to the quantity supplied of the good: Q*. Only at P* there is no more pressure for the price of the good to further change: the market is in *equilibrium*.

This dynamic of the price in response to shortages or surpluses of any good/ service is known as the *<u>price adjustment mechanism</u>*, or, simply, the *<u>market mechanism</u>*. Assuming *ceteris paribus*, it can be summarized as follows:

- if there is a shortage of the good (for whatever reason), the price of the good increases
- if you notice that the price of a good is increasing, then there must be a shortage of the good
- if there is a surplus of the good (for whatever reason), the price of the good decreases
- if you notice that the price of a good is decreasing, then there must be a surplus of the good

■ ■ ■

Practice exercise

What may cause shortages and/or surpluses? Draw a graph of a hypothetical market for, say, chicken, and assume that the market is initially in equilibrium. Mark your P* and Q*. Explain graphically and verbally the overall effect on the market for chicken of the following events:

1. consumers' income increases, *ceteris paribus*
2. there is technological improvement in the "production" of chicken, *ceteris paribus*
3. wages increase, *ceteris paribus*
4. the price of beef decreases, *ceteris paribus*
5. more and more people become vegetarian, *ceteris paribus*

■ ■ ■

Algebraic determination of the market equilibrium

Given that our market demand and supply have algebraic expressions, we can use their equations to find the numerical value of the equilibrium price. In the earlier examples, we had:

Market Demand: $P = 100 - 0.5Q$

Market Supply: $P = 10 + Q$

We find the equilibrium price by finding the intersection between the two lines (Figure 3.13). At the intersection, the value of "P" in the demand must be equal to the value of "P" in the supply, i.e.:

$100 - 0.5Q = 10 + Q$

$1.5Q = 90$

$Q^* = 60$ equilibrium quantity demanded and supplied

$P^* = 70$ equilibrium price

FIGURE 3.13 Graphical representation of the market equilibrium

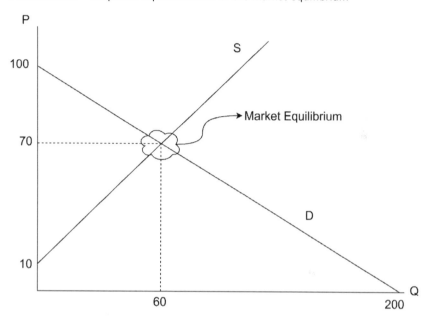

 ## 3.5 Government interventions: *price floors* and *price ceilings*

Sometimes a market's equilibrium price and quantity may be seen as inequitable or not meeting social needs. Government regulation may then be seen as a complement to the market's operation. One such intervention may be through *price controls*. Controls can stipulate a *price ceiling*, i.e. a <u>maximum</u> price, at which a good/service can be <u>legally</u> bought and sold, or a *price floor*, i.e. a <u>minimum</u> price at which a good/service can be <u>legally</u> bought and sold. A good example of a <u>price ceiling</u> is given by the controls on electricity prices in Venezuela, where prices have been kept low in order to help the poor have access to electricity. A good example of a <u>price floor</u> in the US is the price of sugar, which by law cannot fall below a certain level.

A *price ceiling*, seen in Figure 3.14, is effective only in situations of excess demand of a good, as those are the only situations in which the price would

FIGURE 3.14   Graphical representation of an effective *price ceiling*

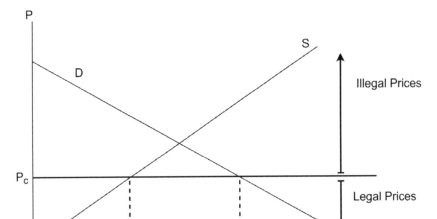

tend to increase. Thus, <u>a price ceiling somehow locks a market in a situation of excess demand</u>. Is this a good thing? Yes and no … on one side, some consumers will be able to obtain the good at an affordable price. On the other, persistent shortages can lead to the development of *black markets*, illegal, parallel markets where the good is exchanged at the actual market price. Persistent shortages are also often accompanied by long lines at the stores, as consumers hope to be "among the first ones" to obtain the limited amount of the good. Finally, price ceilings are often responsible for a deterioration of the quality of the good: this is the effect that the Venezuelan price ceiling has had, as the utility invested in fewer power plants, leading to widespread blackouts.

A *price floor*, represented in Figure 3.15, is effective only in situations of excess supply of a good, as those are the only situations in which the price would tend to decrease. Thus, <u>a price floor locks a market in a situation of excess supply</u>. Again, is this a good thing? Price floors are used both in the US and in the European Union to sustain agricultural prices – and so farmers' income. Typically, governments intervene by buying the excess supply of sugar, corn, tomatoes, and so on (which are stored, if possible, or simply destroyed) to eliminate the pressure on the respective prices to (illegally) decrease below the price floor. On one side, farmers' incomes are sustained. On the other, the government needs to use tax money to purchase these products, and the market price of these products remains higher than it could be for all consumers.

FIGURE 3.15   Graphical representation of an effective *price floor*

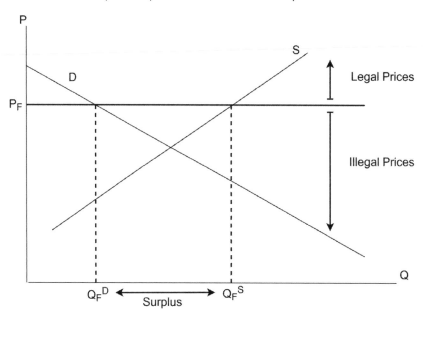

■ ■ ■

Practice exercise

Draw demand, supply, and find market equilibrium given:

D: $P = 10 - 0.05Q_D$
S: $P = 1 + 0.01Q_S$

[You should obtain: $Q^* = 150$, $P^* = 2.5$]

Then describe graphically and verbally the full effects of a price ceiling $P_C = 1$ in this market. How much shortage or surplus does this price ceiling cause?

Opportunity for further reflection: You have already done quite a bit of analytical work in this chapter, and this may be a good moment to reflect on the *power* markets may have acquired on our moral sense, on the moral norms that may be prevalent in society. You may be well aware, out of your own experience, that the market mechanism has reached the most remote aspects of our lives: for instance, schools sometime give monetary incentives to children who complete their homework, or read a book; permits to pollute air, water, and land are bought and sold by firms around the world, and so on. Even *procreation permits* may be tradable! The following insight dialogue, the same type of in-class exercise proposed in Chapter 1, will give you and your classmates the opportunity to internalize the effects that markets may have in aspects of our human and social existence that have historically been kept separate from the logic of costs and benefits.

Insight Dialogue 2

Instructions

All students need a partner in this exercise (the person on your right or on your left): connect for a moment with your partner. If you have not met your partner before, take a moment to introduce yourself. The instructor will take care of timekeeping, so there is no need for you to check your watch.

First 2 minutes: As the instructor signals the beginning of the exercise, immediately start reading the excerpts on the other side of this page. Read carefully and swiftly, noticing what grabs your interest and makes you react the most. Feel free to underline, highlight, etc.

Next 2 minutes: At the instructor's signal, stop reading. Turn your attention inward and notice your personal reaction to what you read. What do you remember the most? Perhaps one excerpt had more effect on you than the others? Notice all that comes to mind ... thoughts, emotions, memories. Stay with what comes up ... do not worry about making your thoughts pretty, or acceptable!

Next 2 minutes: Again, at the instructor's signal, the first person of the pair talks continuously and expresses emotions, sensations, thoughts, memories, words triggered by the excerpts -without editing! The listener just witnesses/listens attentively: no speaking, nodding, making faces ... whatsoever (it is NOT a conversation). Thus, it is not a matter of agreeing or not, or of sounding deep or educated or sophisticated; it is a matter of expressing whatever awareness the speaker has in the moment, and of being deeply listened to.

Next 2 minutes: At the signal, switch person.

Next 2 minutes: When the instructor signals the end of the "dialogue," go back to silence. Perhaps close your eyes, and notice what changed in your thinking or reaction to the excerpts after you spoke and after you listened ...

From: Michael J. Sandel's *What Money Can't Buy. The Moral Limits of Markets*, 2012, p. 70.[2]

In 1964, the economist Kenneth Boulding proposed a system of marketable procreation licenses as a way of dealing with overpopulation. Each woman would be issued a certificate (or two, depending on the policy) entitling her to have a child. She would be free to use the certificate or sell it at the going rate. Boulding imagined a market in which people eager to have children would purchase certificates from (as he indelicately put it) 'the poor, the nuns, the maiden aunts, and so on'.

The plan would be less coercive than a system of fixed quotas, as in a one-child policy. It would also be economically more efficient, since it would get the goods (in this case, children) to the consumers most willing to pay for them. Recently, two Belgian economists revived Boulding's proposal. They pointed out that, since the rich would likely buy procreation licenses from the poor, the scheme would have the further advantage of reducing inequality by giving the poor a new source of income.

■ ■ ■

▨ 3.6 Market failures: public goods and externalities

Our analysis of markets has so far suggested that they are generally the best way to allocate goods and services in society since attempting to set prices above or below equilibrium can result in surpluses or shortages, respectively, of a good or service. However, there are cases in which we might *not* expect markets to result in the "best" level of production, for a number of reasons. The degree to which people believe market failures occur – are they relatively common or relatively rare? – tends to reflect and shape their beliefs about what the relationship between government and markets should be.

Think of important things that the government is tasked with providing: education, infrastructure, national defense, and health care (to some extent). It regulates things like pollution. Would these things be better produced or regulated through markets alone? Most economists agree that they would not.

One case in which markets would fail to achieve the best possible allocation is given by the provision of public goods. A *public good* is one that is <u>non-exclusive</u> (it is difficult to keep people who do not pay from consuming or getting some benefit from the good) and <u>non-rivalrous</u> (my enjoyment of the good does not reduce or impact your ability to benefit from the good). Take the case of national defense, often cited as the quintessential public good.

Countries fund their militaries through the government. What do you think would happen if we left it up to the market to provide this funding? We all enjoy the benefits, but you can enjoy them without paying anything. Would you voluntarily contribute to military funding? If you would contribute, how would you estimate your benefits from the services provided by the military? Even if you could estimate these benefits, would you contribute exactly that amount? Most people would not – and this would lead the military to be under-funded – a problem that is known as the *free-rider* problem. The same issue arises with education and infrastructure spending.

Another case in which markets might not produce the best outcome arises when <u>*externalities*</u> are present. Imagine you purchase a product that is made in a factory that sits on a river. The seller of the good produces and sets the price according to their costs, and you purchase the good based on your willingness to pay (i.e. the benefits you gain from the product). But what if the production results in toxic waste that the factory dumps in the river, traveling downstream and making other people sick? These people pay a cost through reduced well-being, additional spending on health care, and missed days of work, but they are left entirely out of the transaction between you and the factory owner. That is, the cost that they pay is *external* to the transaction that we just modelled in the supply and demand framework above.

FIGURE 3.16   Externalities

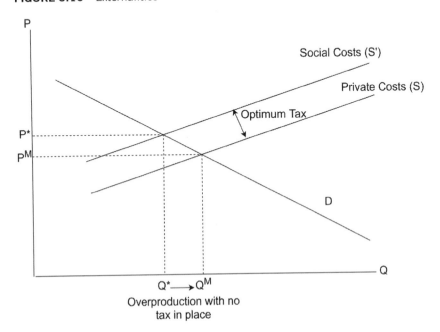

To remedy this, economists argue that external costs should be *internalized* by identifying the amount of damage caused by each unit of production and instituting a tax on the good or service for that amount. This is known as a *Pigouvian tax,* named after A.C. Pigou, the British economist who first proposed it in the early twentieth century. The cost of production *plus* the other costs to society of that production is known as the *social cost,* and it simply adds to the costs of production in the supply curve established earlier. As seen in Figure 3.16, the point at which the social cost curve meets the demand curve is the "true" equilibrium point where production should occur: P*, Q*. Without intervention, equilibrium occurs at the point where the *private cost* curve intersects the demand curve, leading to an overproduction of the good or service: P^M, Q^M. This failure to tax pollution appropriately is, according to environmental economists, the primary reason for environmental degradations and problems like climate change. We will return to this issue of environmental sustainability and build on this perspective in Chapter 8.

EXAMPLE

Let's return to the market example discussed earlier; the equations for supply and demand: were given by:

Market demand: $P = 100 - 0.5Q$

Market supply: $P = 10 + Q$

Recall that $P^* = P^M = 70$ and $Q^* = Q^M = 60$. But now, imagine that this represents an industry that is polluting. The damage from the pollution emitted per unit of production is valued at $10/unit.

What is the optimal price and quantity if the costs of pollution are taken into account?

The tax should equal the pollution damage, so it should be $10/unit.

In order to find the best price and quantity in this framework, let's add the pollution cost onto the market supply function. If pollution cost is $10/unit, this makes the social cost function (the "social" supply function):

Social cost: $P = 10 + Q + 10 = 20 + Q$

Now, just solve as before:

$100 - 0.5Q = 20 + Q$

$Q^* = 53.3$

$P^* = 73.3$

As we can see, the good will be more expensive and less of it will be produced, reducing the pollution being released.

■■■

Opportunity for further reflection/discussion

1.   Do you believe that market failures are relatively rare or relatively common? Why or why not? Can you think of some other example?
2.   Another type of market failure is known as *information asymmetry*, where a buyer or seller has important information about the good or service that the other party does not have. Why could that interfere with the functioning of markets in the supply and demand framework we have developed here?

■■■

 ## 3.7 Price elasticity of demand: sensitivity of the quantity demanded of a good to its own price

The study of demand is of great importance in economics for a variety of reasons. For instance, we may want to know the effect of a tax or a subsidy on the quantity demanded of a specific good (how much state revenue would a higher tax on cigarettes produce? By how much would consumption of cigarettes decrease? What would be the effects on imports of steel if we levied a tax, i.e., a *tariff*, on all imported steel? and so on). Firms may also want to know whether increasing or decreasing the price at which they sell a particular good would boost or depress their revenues. Examples abound.

Notice that the question of whether increasing the price at which a firm sells a good would increase the firm's total revenues is not a trivial question. Total revenues (TR) are given by the multiplication of price and quantity:

$$TR = P \times Q \hspace{5cm} (3.3)$$

Because the demand curve is downward sloping, if the firm increases P, then Q will inevitably decrease. So … what is the cumulative effect on total revenues? This type of information, that is, the percentage change in the quantity demanded of a good, when its price increases, say, by 1%, is given by the *price elasticity of the demand*. Thus:

Price elasticity of demand is a measurement of the absolute value of the responsiveness of the quantity demanded of a good to a change in its own price in percentage terms, and *ceteris paribus*. It is denoted with $E_{P,Q}$, and it is always positive!

Consider the following generic market demand in Figure 3.17:

FIGURE 3.17   Generic market demand

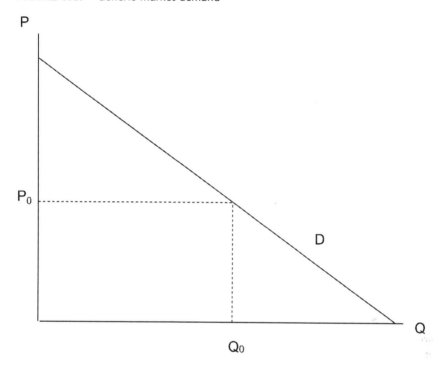

At any given point (P_0, Q_0) of the demand function, the demand is defined as:

- Elastic   if $E_{P,Q} = \left| \dfrac{\%\Delta Q}{\%\Delta P} \right| > 1$

   [as P increases, Total Revenues decrease]

- Unitary Elastic   if $E_{P,Q} = \left| \dfrac{\%\Delta Q}{\%\Delta P} \right| = 1$

   [as P increases, Total Revenues remain the same]

- Inelastic   if $E_{P,Q} = \left| \dfrac{\%\Delta Q}{\%\Delta P} \right| < 1$

   [as P increases, Total Revenues increase]

■ ■ ■

Aside: brief review of "percentage change" (%Δ)

Suppose your weekly allowance increased from $300/week to $400/week: what is the percentage change of your allowance?

$$\%\Delta = \frac{final\ value - initial\ value}{initial\ value} * 100 = \frac{400-300}{300} * 100 = (.33) * 100 = 33\%$$

■ ■ ■

When dealing with a <u>linear demand</u> (as it will always be the case in this text), finding the price elasticity at a specific point of the demand is actually a quite manageable task. Consider the following linear demand:

FIGURE 3.18   Elasticity example

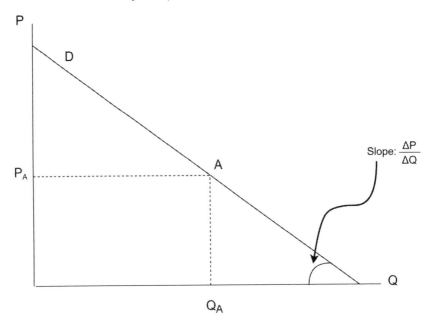

Assume that we want to calculate the price elasticity of this demand at $P = P_A$ and $Q = Q_A$. We want to know, for instance, if, as we increase by 1% the price from P_A, total revenues of the firm selling the good will increase or decrease. Applying the generic %Δ formula presented earlier, our original formula for elasticity reduces to:

$$E_{P,Q} = \left| \frac{\%\Delta Q}{\%\Delta P} \right| = \left| \frac{\frac{\Delta Q}{QA} \times 100}{\frac{\Delta P}{PA} \times 100} \right| \qquad (3.4)$$

i.e.

$$E_{P,Q} = \left| \frac{\Delta Q}{\Delta P} \frac{P_A}{Q_A} \right| \qquad (3.5)$$

Let's now analyze its constituent parts:

- $\frac{\Delta Q}{\Delta P}$: is the inverse of the slope of the demand curve

  Slope: "rise"/"run". Thus, the slope of the demand is $\frac{\Delta P}{\Delta Q}$. Thus, $\frac{\Delta Q}{\Delta P}$ is the inverse of the slope of the demand curve. Example: if the slope of the demand is (-5), then $\frac{\Delta Q}{\Delta P}$ is $(-1/5)]$

- $\frac{P_A}{Q_A}$: P_A and Q_A are the coordinates of the point of the demand where the measurement of the elasticity is made.

Thus, the elasticity on a linear demand can be calculated as the product between the inverse of the slope and the coordinates of the point of measurement.

EXAMPLE

Given the demand function: $P = -.5Q + 100$, determine the value of the price elasticity of the demand at $P_0 = 40$.

Recall that: $E_{P,Q} = \left| \frac{\Delta Q}{\Delta P} \frac{P_0}{Q_0} \right|$.

- $\frac{\Delta Q}{\Delta P} = $ inverse of the slope $= -2$

- $\frac{P_0}{Q_0} = \frac{40}{Q_0}$

To find Q_0, plug $P_0 = 40$ in the demand function, and find the corresponding Q: $40 = -.5Q + 100$, and thus: $Q_0 = 120$

Substitute the values found in the elasticity formula:

$$E_{P,Q} = \left| \frac{\Delta Q}{\Delta P} \frac{P_0}{Q_0} \right| = \left| -2 \frac{40}{120} \right| = \frac{2}{3} = .66\%$$

The demand is *inelastic* at $P_0 = 40$: if the price increases by 1%, the quantity demanded decreases by .66%. Because, in percentage terms, the quantity demanded decreases by less (in absolute value) than the increase in the price, if the firm increases the price from $P_0 = 40$, total revenues increase.

■■■

Practice exercise 1

Given the demand function $P = -4Q + 60$, determine the value of the price elasticity at the following prices:

1) $P = 10$ (you should obtain E = 1/5)
2) $P = 20$ (you should obtain E = 1/2)
3) $P = 40$.   (you should obtain E = 2)

Also state whether, at each of the above points, the demand is *elastic, unitary elastic,* or *inelastic.*

Practice exercise 2

Given the following demand function:

$P = -2Q + 100$

Draw the demand function. Calculate the price elasticity of the demand at: $Q = 1$, $Q = 25$, $Q = 49$ and on each occasion determine whether the demand is elastic, unitary elastic, or inelastic. Show all your calculations.

■■■

3.8 Income elasticity of demand

The measurement of the responsiveness of the quantity demanded to changes in income (again, expressed in percentage terms) can be similarly defined:

Income elasticity of the demand measures the responsiveness of the quantity demanded to a change in income, in percentage terms, and *ceteris paribus.* It is expressed in a now familiar expression:

$$E_{I,Q} = \frac{\%\Delta Q}{\%\Delta I} = \frac{\Delta Q}{\Delta P} \frac{I_0}{Q_0} \tag{3.6}$$

Notice the absence of absolute value: the income elasticity of demand can, in fact, be positive or negative.

- If $E_{I,Q} > 0$ the good is perceived as _normal_: as income increases (decreases), the quantity demanded of the good increases (decreases) – numerator and denominator have the same sign.
- If $E_{I,Q} < 0$ the good is perceived as _inferior_: as income increases (decreases), the quantity demanded of the good decreases (increases) – numerator and denominator have opposite signs.

As we saw in Figures 3.3 and 3.4, these distinctions are important.

Notes

1. Crop Values Annual Summary, https://afdc.energy.gov/data/10338.
2. Michael J. Sandel is the Anne T. and Robert M. Bass Professor of Government at Harvard University. Author of several books on ethics and markets, his writings have been translated into 18 languages; in 2010, *China Newsweek* named him "the most influential foreign figure of the year" in China.

Reference

Sandel, Michael J. (2012) *What Money Can't Buy. The Moral Limits of Markets*. New York: Farrar, Strauss and Giroux.

4

Inside the magic box

Productivity, costs, and profit maximization

 ## 4.1 Introduction to the Neoclassical firm: the production function

We now turn to the "individual agent" of the supply side to understand a bit more deeply where the positive relationship between the price of a good and quantity supplied of a good comes from and, specifically, the role that technology and costs of inputs play in determining such relationship. So we start from the individual supplier of a good or service that we call: the *firm*.

In general, for our purposes, a *firm* is an *organization* that *produces* goods and services. Given such definition, a firm can be studied either as an *organization*, or as a *production facility*. When we emphasize the *organizational* aspects of a firm, we focus on power relationships, organization of the work-force in relationship to technology, ownership of and relationships among factors of production, communication and organizational possibilities, which leads to what is typically considered a Marxist analysis of the firm, and to a sociological interpretation of the norms that support (or potentially undermine) production activities. We will not delve into these topics in this book.

The way we look at the firm in this book refers to what is known as the *Neoclassical firm*; that is, an entity whose specific *function* is *production* and whose specific *objective is the maximization of profits*. It is thus a more technological, mathematical, engineering-like way of looking at the firm than the approach described in the previous paragraph. In this light, we may think of a firm as some sort of *magic box*: inputs enter the box, where they find a technology that combines them efficiently and transforms them into output – which is what comes out of the box. *The box itself is the firm.* So, a definition that better describes the way we analyze the firm might be the following: <u>the firm is a particular technology that efficiently transforms inputs into output with the objective of maximizing profits</u>. Schematically:

Notice that this is a view of the firm that completely mimics the mathematical concept of a *function*: inputs are independent variables; technology is the mathematical function (what we will call the production function) that determines how these inputs can be efficiently combined; and output (the good or service that the firm produces) is the dependent variable.

For instance, if the firm is a hair salon that produces haircuts:

- Inputs: amounts of labor, capital (tools, space, and so on), say per month
- Output: number of haircuts per month
- Production function (i.e., the *technology*, i.e., the *firm*): the number of haircuts per month is a function of the amount of labor and capital the firm hires/rents per month and the specific ways haircuts are performed at the hair-salon.

In general, if we indicate with **L** the amount of labor, with **K** the amount of capital, and with **Q** the amount of output, the production activity of the firm is fully described by:

$$Q = F(K, L) \quad \text{PRODUCTION FUNCTION} \tag{4.1}$$

where F(K, L) is the mathematical function that represents the technology utilized by the firm.

Particular attention needs to be given to the specific meaning of the word "capital" in this context: "capital" stands for capital stock, that is, machinery, tools, space, and any durable element that is actively used in the production process. It does not refer to pure financial capital.

So, for instance, what do we understand from a production function such as $Q = K + 2L$? We understand that if, say, 1 unit of capital and 3 units of labor enter the *magic box* (the production function, that is, the firm), 7 units of output will be obtained from the *magic box* (that is, will be efficiently produced: to see this, substitute $K = 1$ and $L = 3$ in $Q = K + 2L$, and calculate Q). We also understand that this output could be produced by utilizing only K, or only L, or some combination of the two: thus, this is a technology that allows production to happen in completely automatized ways (only K used; zero labor), or completely by hand (only L used; zero capital), or through some combination of machinery and labor. A car-wash could be an example of a firm that may use this type of technology.

Of course, there may be many more than two types of inputs: the type of analysis would not change, it would just become mathematically more complex. In this text, we'll keep it as simple as possible, and we'll consider only two inputs: capital and labor.

4.2 Short-run vs. long-run in production

In microeconomics we distinguish a *long-run* from a *short-run* timeframe when we study the production side of the economy.

When the firm makes decisions with a sufficiently extended time horizon so that there is time to optimize both capital and labor when deciding how to produce a certain quantity of output, we say that the firm operates in a *long-run* framework. Thus, given any specific quantity of output the firm wants to produce, *in the long-run, a firm will always be able to choose the optimal level of both capital and labor*, that is, the combination of inputs that minimizes the costs of production of that particular level of output.

We instead say that the firm operates in a *short-run* framework when the time horizon is such that there is not sufficient time to change all inputs. Thus, in the short-run at least one of the inputs is fixed (typically, the level of capital is fixed, as changing the level of capital, i.e., machinery or space, requires more time than changing the amount of labor employed), and the firm can produce different quantities only by changing the level of labor. Thus, *in the short-run, the firm's choice of how to produce any given level of output is constrained by a fixed amount of capital*. In general, because of this constraint, the firm will not be able to produce different quantities of output at the minimum possible cost.

Short-run and *long-run* do refer to "time," but do not refer to a set amount of time appropriate to all types of firms: the time horizon that identifies *short-run* and *long-run* really depends on the type of activity under consideration. For instance, the time needed for a technologically very sophisticated and large firm, say, Boeing, to change the level of machinery (K) used in production is much longer than the time required, for example, for the cafeteria of your university to modify its capital stock. Thus, "short-run" for Boeing is a much longer period of time than for the cafeteria.

The most intuitive way to think about the long-run is to think about the timeframe one has when one sets up a firm from scratch: everything needs to be decided, and there is the freedom of adopting the level of K that seems most appropriate for the average amount of output one foresees for the firm. Once K is set and the firm begins to operate, the firm will need to be managed on a day-by-day basis in the short-run timeframe, as K has become fixed (for instance, for the duration of lease contracts of machinery or space). On a day-by-day basis, the firm will be able to fulfill whatever is the needed level of production only by changing the amount of labor.

4.3 Short-run profit maximization: concepts of *economic* and *normal* profits

As established at the beginning of this chapter, the objective of the Neoclassical firm is the maximization of profits, that is, the maximization of the difference between *total revenues* (TR) and *total costs* (TC). Total revenues are straightforward: they consist of the "money" the firm receives from the sale of its output: if the firm produces loaves of bread, total revenues are calculated by multiplying the number of loaves of bread produced (and sold) by their sale price. Total costs are a bit more nuanced, as they are calculated differently depending on whether we are calculating *accounting profits* or *economic profits*. When we calculate *accounting profits* (for instance, to figure out the amount of taxes the firm owes), total costs consist of the "money" spent on capital, labor, and any other input that has been used to achieve the amount of output produced by the firm. When we calculate *economic profits*, we add the *opportunity cost* of utilizing all the employed resources for this particular enterprise (rather than their alternative best use) and the total costs listed above (the total costs calculated to figure out accounting profits). Thus, if by producing a certain number of loaves of bread you lose the *opportunity* of making profits by producing cookies instead, that *loss* needs to be added to the total costs seen earlier. Using the Greek Pi (Π) to indicate economic profits, we have:

$$\Pi = TR - TC \quad \text{where TC also includes the opportunity cost.} \qquad (4.2)$$

The firm is said to obtain:

- <u>economic profits</u> when $\Pi > 0$, i.e. TR > TC
- <u>normal profits</u> when $\Pi = 0$, i.e. TR = TC;
- <u>economic losses</u> when $\Pi < 0$, i.e. TR < TC.

"Normal" profit is the situation in which a firm "breaks even." Notice that in this situation all costs, including the opportunity cost, are fully covered by the firm's revenues. More specifically, in this situation <u>every input</u> gets fully paid at the current rates or wages. You may wonder: why bother to own this firm if the firm is just breaking even? Well, if the owner of the firm owns all or part of the capital stock (machinery, space, and so on), then the owner will receive a normal return from the investment in that capital stock. And if the owner actually works in the firm, the owner will also receive the appropriate compensation for her/his labor. The firm just "makes enough" to cover all the costs without losing and without gaining anything extra (no economic losses, no economic profits).

Take a moment to reflect on these different concepts of profits. What does it mean to a firm's operation if it is not making a normal profit? Now, how would you describe the other profit situations?

▋ 4.4 A survey of market structures

In order to analyze the decision-making process that leads to the firm's maximization of profits, we need to become very well acquainted with the determinants of Total Revenues and Total Costs.

Let's begin our analysis with total revenues. We have already encountered this concept when we talked about the price elasticity of demand in Chapter 3: total revenues consist of the "money" the firm obtains by selling its output, i.e., $TR = P * Q$, where "P" is the price of each unit of output, and "Q" is the firm's output. Thus, if the firm is a hair salon that produced 200 haircuts (Q = 200) sold at \$30 each (P = \$30), the total revenues of the hair salon turns out to be \$6,000.

A key question we need to look at is: if the firm changes the quantity produced, does the firm affect/change the price at which that quantity produced can be sold? Another way to ask this question is: does the price at which the firm can sell its product depend on how many units of the product the firm brings to the market? What is your intuition about this? If Apple doubles the number of iPhones supplied in the market, do you think that the price of iPhones will be affected? If a peasant with a small number of cows doubles the amount of milk supplied in the overall market of milk, do you think that the price of milk would be affected?

You may have already come to the realization that the answer to these questions depends on *how large the firm is in relationship to the market* in which the firm operates. If the firm is one of the many that supply exactly the same product to the market, the quantity produced by the single firm is too small to be "felt" by the market. In this case, a single firm's decision to change the quantity produced will not affect the market price of that particular product. If, on the other hand, the firm is perhaps the only one producing the specific good (in this case, the firm would be a monopolist), then any change in the quantity produced by the firm will certainly be felt by the market, and thus a change in the quantity produced will affect the market price.

The number of firms participating in any given market, and thus the degree of competition existing in any given market, gives rise to what we call *market structure*.

The most important market structures, from the most to the least competitive, are:

1. *Perfect competition*: many, many firms in the market, producing the same product; this is a benchmark, highly abstract case;
2. *Monopolistic competition*: many, many firms in the market, producing differentiated products; for instance: cereals;
3. *Oligopoly*: a relatively small number of firms producing the same product; for instance: laptops;

4. *Duopoly*: only two firms in the market, producing the same product; for instance: Boeing and Airbus;
5. *Monopoly*: only one firm in the market; for instance: your gas company.

In this introductory text, we will only discuss "the most" and "the least" competitive market structures: perfect competition first, and monopoly later.

4.5 Total revenues for the perfectly competitive firm

Perfect competition is an extreme case of "extreme" competition, rarely seen in real life, but an excellent theoretical benchmark for a number of insights and analytical relationships that help us describe the "supply side" of the economy.
   Perfect competition is defined as a market characterized by:

*   a homogeneous (non-differentiated) product; no need for advertising, as everybody sells exactly the same thing (milk used to be a great example; in the last few years it has become a differentiated product, and thus a monopolistic competitive market)
*   a very large number of buyers and sellers in the market, so that no one can individually influence the price of the product: each consumer and supplier is a <u>price-taker</u>, that is, each takes the market price of the good as given
*   great fluidity of firms and consumers, with free and costless entry and exit of consumers and firms in the market (no requirements such as licensing and so on)
*   every firm has perfect and equal information on prices of inputs, technology, and so on.

In perfect competition the price of the product is determined by the cumulative interaction of *all producers* and *all consumers*. We already learned how that happens in the study of the *market* and the derivation of the equilibrium price discussed in Chapter 3. The equilibrium price in the market (intersection of market demand and supply) is the price that <u>perfectly competitive firms take as given</u>. Then, at that price, the firm has to determine the quantity to produce that will maximize its profits. This is like saying that the demand for the single perfectly competitive firm is perfectly horizontal at the equilibrium price: at that price, the single firm can sell as much or little as the firm chooses without affecting the market price (Figure 4.1). The problem is to identify that particular quantity of output that maximizes profits.
   Recall the initial question we asked when we discussed total revenues: does the quantity produced by the firm affect/change the price at which that quantity produced can be sold? In perfect competition the answer is: NO! In

FIGURE 4.1   Market equilibrium and demand for the perfectly competitive firm

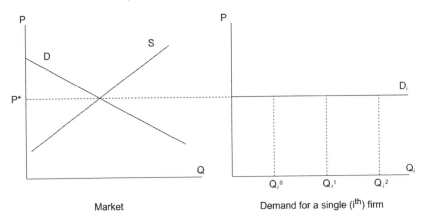

Market   Demand for a single (i^{th}) firm

perfect competition the price is given by the market and does not depend on
how much a single firm produces.

4.6 Building block of short-run cost analysis: marginal productivity of labor

Recall the production function $Q = F (K, L)$, and the concept of short-run (at
least one input is fixed: capital). We have already seen that the way K is chosen
has to do with the average amount of output the firm expects to produce in
the long-run. Thus, in the short-run the production function becomes:

$$Q = F (K_{Fixed}, L) \tag{4.3}$$

that is, in the short-run, Q is only a function of L (K is a given, fixed number).

EXAMPLE

Earlier, we discussed the production function $Q = K + 2L$. Suppose that
K has been fixed at $K_0 = 100$. The short-run production function then is:
$Q = 100 + 2L$ (Q is only a function of L).

Think, for instance, about the cafeteria at your university: its capital stock,
K, (tables, space, counter space, kitchen tools and machines, ovens, refrig-
erators, and so on) has been determined in the past, with a certain student
population in mind, and thus a certain number of meals to be produced per
day. Given the chosen level of K and the then-foreseen number of meals to
be produced per day, a certain number of workers (L) would have also been
ideal. But ... the student population varies every year, actually every semester,

which implies that the number of meals that end up being produced day after day is never exactly equal to the number of meals that was envisioned when the level of K was originally decided.

In the short-run, depending on the number of meals produced every day, while capital (K) stays fixed at its value, different amounts of labor (L) are employed. So, given the fixed amount of capital, it becomes really important for the firm to know how additional units of labor (say, additional employees) affect the amount of output obtained. The additional output obtained by employing one additional unit of labor, given a fixed level of capital, is called marginal productivity of labor (MPL). In symbols:

$$MPL = \frac{\Delta Q}{\Delta L} \quad \text{(read: "change in output obtained by employing one additional unit of labor")} \quad (4.4)$$

Let's see what the MPL really means through a numerical example. Complete the table in Practice Exercise 4.1.

By looking at Figure 4.2, you will notice the increasing and then decreasing pattern of the MPL. Starting from L = 0, as the number of workers becomes closer and closer to the number of workers that would be "ideal" (L*) for the fixed amount of capital, the MPL increases: each additional worker is more productive than the previous one, as each additional worker can take better and better advantage of the existing capital. This is the process of *specialization* of labor, and, in this region, the firm is said to be characterized by increasing marginal productivity of labor. Once labor reaches a number higher than the number of workers that would be "ideal" for the fixed

PRACTICE EXERCISE 4.1   Calculation of the marginal productivity of labor (Remember: K is fixed in the short-run)

Workers (L)	# Meals (Q)	#Meals prepared by each additional worker: $MPL = \frac{\Delta Q}{\Delta L}$
0	0	
1	10	
2	25	
3	80	
4	180	
5	300	
6	500	
7 (ideal given K)	800	
8	1,000	
9	1,150	
10	1,250	
11	1,300	
12	1,320	

amount of capital, the MPL begins to decrease. Each additional worker is less productive than the previous one, as all the specialization opportunities have already been utilized, and each additional worker can only duplicate "jobs" that already exist in the firm. In this region, the firm is said to be characterized by <u>decreasing marginal productivity of labor</u> (or decreasing returns to labor).

FIGURE 4.2   Generic shape of the MPL

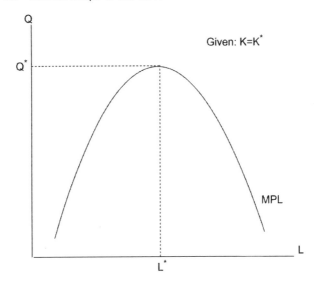

L*: "ideal" number of workers for the level of capital K*.

■ ■ ■

Opportunity for further reflection

Can you imagine a situation in which MPL = 0? Can you imagine a situation in which MPL < 0? If yes, how would you describe these situations?

■ ■ ■

4.7 Short-run cost functions

The initially increasing and then decreasing pattern of the MPL provides us with a great introduction to the pattern of short-run costs.

This description may sound a bit cumbersome, so ... *go slow and follow the logic step by step*! An increasing MPL implies that each additional worker produces more and more units of output than the previous one. Yet, each additional worker is paid the same wage, i.e., costs the same to the firm. This implies that, when the MPL is increasing, the same cost (the wage paid to each additional worker) corresponds to more and more units of output, i.e., when the MPL is increasing each additional unit of output costs to the firm less and less. <u>The additional cost the firm incurs to produce one additional unit of output is a fundamental cost concept here, the *Marginal Cost*</u> (MC):

$$MC = \frac{\Delta\,Total\,Cost}{\Delta Q}$$ (read: "change in total cost due to the production of one more unit of output")   (4.5)

FIGURE 4.3   Patterns of MPL and MC

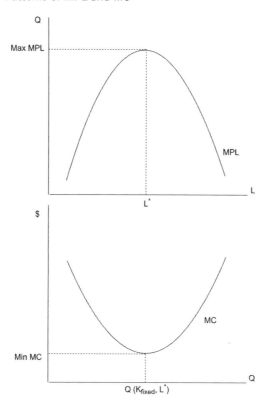

You may want to try to follow a symmetrical argument to show that when the MPL is decreasing, the MC has to be increasing.

Important: notice that the horizontal axis in the MPL graph (Figure 4.2) is "units of labor" (L), while the horizontal axis in the MC graph (Figure 4.3, and all other "cost" graphs) is "quantity produced" (Q) …

There are a number of other concepts of short-run costs for a firm. Given that our firm utilizes only capital K and labor L, the total cost of the firm will be the sum of the cost of capital and the cost of labor. Capital is assumed as rented at a known unitary rental rate (symbol: "r"), while labor is compensated at the prevailing wage (symbol: "w").

Thus:

$$Total\ Cost = TC = r\ K_{Fixed} + w\ L \tag{4.6}$$

Given that the cost of capital is fixed in the short-run, the cost of capital is known as *Fixed Cost* (FC), while the cost of labor is known as the *Variable Cost* (VC).

Thus, we have:

$$TC = FC + VC \tag{4.7}$$

where

$$FC = r\ K_{Fixed} \tag{4.8}$$

$$VC = w\ L \tag{4.9}$$

If we divide the left- and right-hand side of the equality $TC = FC + VC$ by "Q", the amount of output produced, we then obtained the total, fixed, and variable costs *per unit of output produced*. These concepts go under the names of: *Average Cost* (AC), *Average Fixed Cost* (AFC), and *Average Variable Cost* (AVC).

$$AC = \frac{TC}{Q} \tag{4.10}$$

$$AFC = \frac{FC}{Q} \tag{4.11}$$

$$AVC = \frac{VC}{Q} \tag{4.12}$$

Notice that:

$$AC = AVC + AFC \qquad \text{always!} \tag{4.13}$$

And, finally, let's bring back *marginal cost*. Remember, it's equal to the change in total cost (or, equivalently, the change in the variable cost, as K is fixed, and so its cost does not change when the quantity produced changes) incurred when one more unit of output is produced:

$$MC = \frac{\Delta TC}{\Delta Q} = \frac{\Delta VC}{\Delta Q} \qquad\qquad (4.14)$$

You should now be ready to apply these concepts to some numbers.

▨ Practice exercise 4.2: Calculations of all short-run costs

The solution of Practice exercise 4.1 should have given you the values of the MPL at the various levels of Labor employed and the number of meals produced. You are now asked to connect those results to the corresponding costs. The following is a summary of the cost functions introduced in this section.

Fixed Cost:	FC = Rental Rate*K
Average Fixed Cost:	AFC = FC/Q
Variable Cost of all meals produced:	VC = Wage*L
Total Cost of all meals produced:	TC = FC + VC
Marginal Cost of a meal:	MC = ΔVC/ΔQ
Average Variable Cost of a meal:	AVC = VC/Q
Average Cost of a meal:	AC = AVC + AFC

Fill out the following table, assuming that the wage (per day) = $100, and that the fixed costs are $5,000. From your answers construct a graph of the MC, with MC ($) on the vertical axis and Q on the horizontal axis.

PRACTICE EXERCISE 4.2 Calculations of all short-run costs

L	Q	MPL	VC	TC	AVC	AC	MC
0	0	–					
1	10	10					
2	25	15					
3	80	55					
4	180	100					
5	300	120					
6	500	200					
7	800	300					
8	1,000	200					
9	1,150	150					
10	1,250	100					
11	1,300	50					
12	1,320	20					

Graphical representation of short-run cost functions

Let's bring back the generic graph of the marginal cost. Does your graph in Practice Exercise 4.2 look similar to Figure 4.4?

FIGURE 4.4   Marginal cost, once again

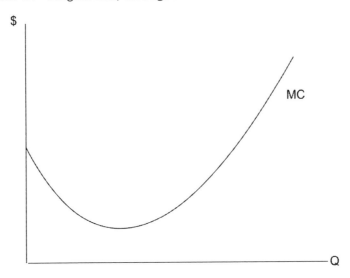

Now let's add to Figure 4.4 the generic patterns of the AVC and the AC (Figure 4.5). Let's reflect first on the relationship between "marginal" and "average" values. Think about your GPA (the "average" grade), and let's proceed from the very first grade you received at the end of the first semester of your first year (if this is your first semester in college, try to work with your imagination!): if your marginal grade is decreasing (that is, the second grade you received is lower than the first but higher than the third, and so on), what must be true of your GPA? Your GPA would be: 1) decreasing, and 2) always higher than your marginal grade. This is the case whenever you compare "marginal" and "average" concepts!

So, let's apply this logic to costs: starting from Q = 0, as the MC decreases, the AVC and AC will have to be decreasing but higher than the MC. In addition, remember that AC = AFC + AVC, and thus the AC must also always be higher than the AVC; yet, because the AFC decreases as Q increases (for instance, FC/2 is a much bigger number than FC/1,000), the difference between AC and AVC becomes smaller and smaller as Q increases.

Now, reflect on the following: as we said, if the marginal is lower than the average, the average must be decreasing. Because AVC and AC are decreasing and higher than the MC, and because the MC is U-shaped, it must be

FIGURE 4.5 Average variable cost and average cost from marginal cost: first step

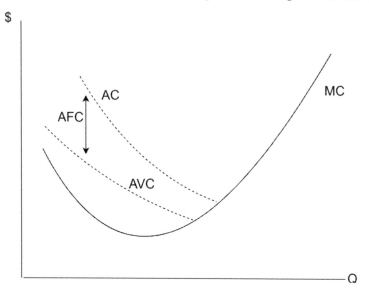

that at some point the AVC and AC cross the MC. Once each crosses the MC, as Q further increases the marginal becomes larger than the average, and therefore the average (both AVC and AC) must become increasing. Thus, it can only be that AVC and AC must reach their minimum value when they intersect (at the intersection with) the MC! These patterns are represented in Figure 4.6.

FIGURE 4.6 Full representation of short-run cost curves

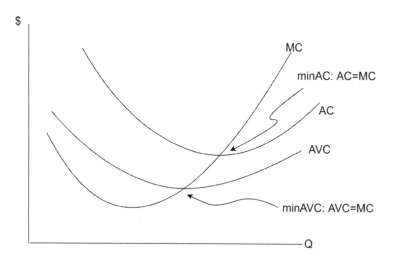

▉ 4.8 Profit maximization in perfect competition (short-run)

We are now ready to bring together revenues and costs and construct the thought process that should guide a perfectly competitive firm in its profit maximization. As we have seen earlier, a perfectly competitive firm has no control on the market price but has full control of its own level of production Q_i (careful with the symbols! Q_i is now the quantity produced by individual firm "i"). Thus, <u>profit maximization for a competitive firm means *choosing the quantity to produce Q_i that maximizes the firm's profits*</u>.

The information available in the management office of the firm is the following:

FIGURE 4.7   Information available to the perfectly competitive firm (choice of level of output)

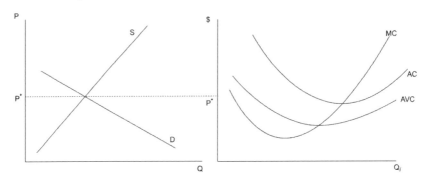

How much should the firm produce in order to maximize profits, i.e., maximize the difference between total revenues and total costs?

In Figure 4.8, pick quantity Q_i^A as a starting point: would the firm's profits increase if the firm slightly increases production from Q_i^A? Yes! An additional unit would sell for a price higher than the cost of producing it (MC), thus leading to additional profit (on that additional unit beyond Q_i^A). Thus, if the MC is lower than the price P, the firm should always increase production in order to increase profits. In other words, the firm would lose profit opportunities if it produced a quantity at which the MC is lower than the price.

Consider now quantity Q_i^B: would the firm's profits increase if the firm slightly decreases production from Q_i^B? Yes! Decreasing production by one unit would eliminate the loss the firm incurs in the production of the unit Q_i^B, thus increasing overall profits. Thus, if the MC is higher than the price P, the firm should always decrease production in order to increase profits.

FIGURE 4.8   Profit maximization: reasoning at the margin

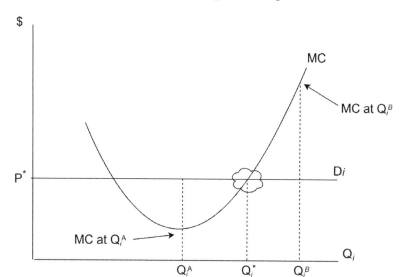

But then it's clear how much the perfectly competitive firm should produce in order to maximize profits: the quantity at which marginal cost is
equal to the price!

- *Golden Rule* for profit maximization in perfect competition:
  Produce at Q_i^* so that $MC = P$ (4.15)

Generalization of the *Golden Rule* for profit maximization (every market
structure): choose the quantity of output Q_i^* so that *the additional revenue
the firm obtains by selling the unit Q_i^* (the marginal revenue, symbolized
by MR) is equal to the additional cost the firm incurs to produce the unit
Q_i^* (the marginal cost, MC).* Thus, the generalized Golden Rule for profit
maximization is:

- *Golden Rule* for profit maximization in *any* market structure:
  Produce at Q_i^* so that $MC = MR$ (4.16)

In perfect competition, this condition becomes $P = MC$ because the marginal
revenue, that is, the revenue the firm obtains by selling one more unit of
output, is equal to the market price (the perfectly competitive firm is too
small to affect the market price, and thus its marginal revenue is always equal
to the market price).

We can now visualize the amount of profits made by the firm in the
graph that represents the firm's cost functions. Recall the definition of

profits, and apply the concepts of total revenues and total and average costs to obtain:

$$\Pi = TR - TC = P \times Q_i^* - AC \times Q_i^* = Q_i^* (P - AC) \qquad (4.17)$$

where:

- P comes from the market: it's given and known to the firm;
- Q_i^* is the quantity that maximizes profits (only at Q_i^*: $P = MC$);
- AC is the value of the Average Cost when the firm produces Q_i^*.

Now is, again, a time for reflection. Look at Figures 4.9 and 4.10. Explain why each firm is making positive or negative profits. Determine where a firm would have to operate if it was just breaking even (making normal profits).

FIGURE 4.9   Positive economic profits for the perfectly competitive firm

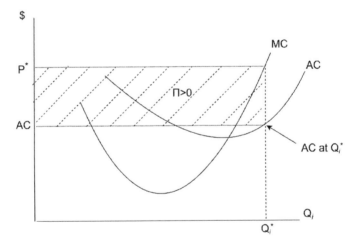

When the price P is lower than the minimum AVC, the firm <u>shuts down</u> in the short-run: $P_{SD} = MC = AVC_{min}$. This is shown in Figure 4.11.

Transition from the short-run to the long-run competitive equilibrium

What happens as we let time go, so that new firms can enter the market or some existing firms enter their "long-run" and can exit the market without carrying fixed costs (as all costs are variable in the long-run[1])?

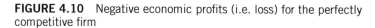

FIGURE 4.10   Negative economic profits (i.e. loss) for the perfectly competitive firm

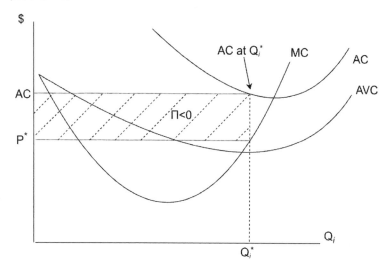

FIGURE 4.11   (Short-run) shut-down price

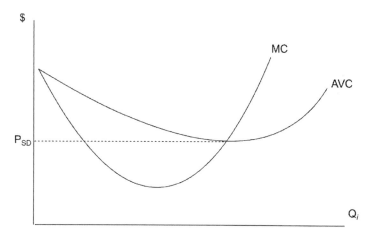

- If the existing firms make positive economic profits, new firms will have an incentive to enter the market. As new firms enter the market, the market supply of the product will shift to the right, causing the equilibrium price to decrease. As the price decreases, existing firms will see their profits decrease. This process will continue until there is no more incentive for new firms to enter the market. At that point, the existing firms will earn zero profits, i.e., the price will have decreased enough so that $P = MC = AC_{minimum}$.

- If the existing firms make negative economic profits (and yet the price is higher than the *shut-down* price), firms will exit the market as soon as they can get rid of their capital stock (i.e., as soon as they individually reach their long-run). As firms begin to exit the market, the market supply of the product will shift to the left, causing the equilibrium price to increase. As the price increases, firms that are still in the market will see their losses (negative profits) decrease. This process will continue until there is no more incentive for any firm to exit the market. At that point, losses (i.e., profits) will be zero, i.e., the price will have decreased enough so that $P = MC = AC_{minimum}$.

Therefore, in the long-run, the price in a perfectly competitive market will have to be:

$$P_{LR} = MC = AC_{minimum}.$$ (4.18)

and profits will be zero.

PRACTICE EXERCISE

Draw a market and a single firm's costs diagram next to each other, as done earlier in this section. Construct it so that the market is in its long-run equilibrium (the intersection of market demand and supply determines a price that is equal to the minimum AC). Profits, therefore, are zero for all the existing firms. Then, imagine that a successful social media campaign increases the market demand for the product. Show on your diagram the shift in the demand, the new equilibrium price, and what happens in the short-run to the existing firms.

4.9 Profit maximization in monopoly

A monopoly is literally the opposite market structure of perfect competition: only one firm produces the product, and no close substitutes of the product exist.

How do monopolies come into being? Some of the reasons for which an industry may become a monopoly are:

- Legal barriers to entry: no other firm can enter the market because of municipal laws (e.g., water), *product* or *process* patents, copyright, and so on.
- Economies of scale (a.k.a. *increasing returns to scale*): if the technology is such that the efficiency of the firm increases with its size, then the

average cost must be decreasing all along. That is, the more a firm produces the lower its average cost is, and thus the lower the price the firm
can charge. The largest firm can kick every other firm out of business!
- Exclusive ownership of essential resources for production (e.g., De
Beers and diamonds in South Africa).

The big difference between monopoly and perfect competition is that the
demand for the product of the monopolist is downward sloping rather than
perfectly horizontal. In a monopoly, the firm alone faces the whole market
demand of the product, and thus the price of the product completely depends
on how many units of the product the firm brings to the market. This implies
that the market price is under the complete control of the monopolist: we say
that a monopolist is a *price-maker*. By determining the level of output, the
monopolist also determines the market price.

So, how many units of the product should a monopolist bring to the market
to maximize profits? Let's bring the market demand and the cost curves on to
the same graph in Figure 4.12.

FIGURE 4.12   Information available to the monopolist (choice of the level of
output)

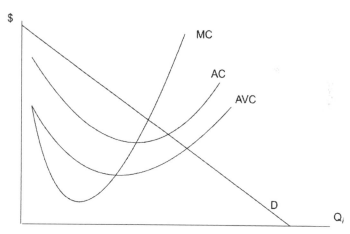

Let's reflect on what we read on the demand function: given a quantity,
say 50 units, the demand tells us the price the firm receives *per unit*, i.e., the
revenue *per unit* received by the firm. Thus, the demand tells us the *average
revenue* obtained by the firm. Now, recall the relationship between "average"
and "marginal" discussed in our treatment of costs (Figures 4.5 and 4.6).
If your GPA is all the way decreasing, what must be true of your marginal
grades relative to your GPA? Your marginal grades must be always lower
than your GPA. We can apply the same reasoning here: given that the *average*

revenue (the demand) is all the way downward sloping, what must be true of the *marginal revenue* relative to the *average revenue*? The marginal revenue must be always lower than the average revenue; that is, it must be always lower than the demand! You can also think of this by thinking that if the monopolist wants to sell more, it has to decrease the price: thus, the additional revenue that comes from one more unit sold must be lower than the price obtained from the previous units.

It so happens that when we have a linear demand function (as is always the case in this text), the marginal revenue bisects the upper angle of the demand. That is, if the demand intersects the horizontal axis at a value *a*, the marginal revenue intersects the horizontal axis at a value *a/2*.

FIGURE 4.13   Linear demand and marginal revenue

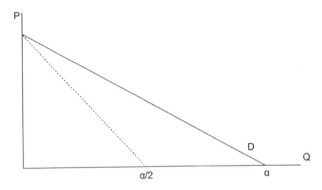

FIGURE 4.14   Profit maximization in monopoly

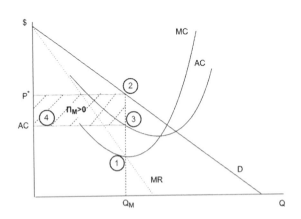

Following the general *golden rule for profit maximization* seen earlier in this section, that is, marginal revenue = marginal cost, the diagram of profit maximization for a monopolist looks like Figure 4.14:

To determine the monopolist's profits, go by the following steps:

1. $MR = MC$ determines Q_M, the quantity produced by the monopolist;
2. from Q_M find P*, the monopolist's price: the demand determines the (highest) price at which Q_M can be sold in the market;
3. from Q_M find the corresponding average cost sustained by the monopolist at Q_M;
4. determine profits by applying the same formula seen in perfect competition:

$$\Pi_M = Q_M (P^* - AC) \tag{4.19}$$

Notice that:

- a monopoly does not have a supply function. Given the demand, there is only one possible quantity supplied: a supply *point*.
- the monopolist's profits are both short-run and long-run: no entry of new firms is possible in a monopoly, so the monopolist's profits remain unchallenged through time.

Suggestions for further discussion

1. Discuss the inefficiency of monopoly relative to perfect competition: the good is not brought to the market at the lowest possible price (which happens when $= AC_{min}$), which leads to a loss for society.
2. Would the public (consumers) gain from governmental intervention to avoid monopolies (antitrust laws)?
3. Do you think monopoly or perfect competition is more likely to lead to innovation and growth?

Note

1. Notice that here we are simplifying the matter a little bit, as we are using the short-run cost curves also for the long-run. Even though the general pattern of the cost curves remains the same, you should be aware that the long-run and the short-run cost curves do not coincide. If you continue to study economics, you will learn how to derive long-run costs in a more advanced microeconomics course.

5 Understanding the wealth of nations

National income accounting

 ## 5.1 Circular flows and fundamental macroeconomic identities

We now need to shift our focus from a *micro* to a *macro* level. In the microeconomics section of the book we paid attention to the behavior of single agents of the economy, specifically the *consumer* and the *producer* (the *firm*). The variables we used were pertinent to these agents: fundamentally the relationships between price and quantity of goods and services, studied from the point of view of consumers and suppliers, respectively.

A macroeconomic *story*, and some macroeconomic vocabulary

When we approach the *macroeconomy*, the aggregate economy of a country, a region, and so on, the functions of the various economic agents change, as agents are not seen only as relating to a specific market but become the integrated engines of the economy taken as a whole.

Thus, <u>households</u> not only demand goods and services, but also supply labor and capital to the production processes of the country. In exchange, they receive income that can be used to purchase consumption goods and services, pay taxes, and add to the households' savings. Households' savings are placed in <u>the financial sector</u>: banks receive savings and turn them around in the form of lending to firms for their <u>investments</u>, i.e., to purchase <u>capital goods</u> that will further their production processes in the future. The amount of lending banks can do out of the savings they receive is regulated by the central bank (the Federal Reserve System in the US), and the economic policy implemented by the central bank of a country is known as *monetary policy*. <u>Firms</u> thus not only produce goods and services purchased by households for consumption; they also produce goods that are purchased by the firms themselves (investments).

We then have the <u>public sector</u> (government), whose economic activity mainly consists of <u>taxation</u>, which diminishes the <u>disposable income</u> of households and represents the government's revenues, and <u>public spending</u> (a.k.a. public expenditure), which contributes to the overall demand of goods and services in the economy. Changes in public spending and/or taxation are the main ways in which *fiscal policy* is implemented by the government of a country. Depending on whether the government's revenues are larger or smaller than public expenditure, the country will respectively be running a *budget surplus* or a *budget deficit*.

And finally, some of the goods and services produced by the country may be bought by entities of other countries (foreign households, firms, or governments), and some of the income generated in the country may be used to buy goods produced in other countries. These are the country's <u>exports and imports</u>, and depending on whether exports are larger or smaller than imports, the country will be respectively running a *trade surplus* or a *trade deficit*.

Summing up, as we approach the study of macroeconomics, we analyze a new set of economic agents:

- Households
- Firms
- Financial sector (banks)
- Government
- Rest of the world

The macroeconomic relationships among all these agents can be schematically described by so-called flow charts that show an economy as an organic system of flows of expenditures, income, and production. You may find it interesting to know that the first study of these economic flows was performed in the eighteenth century by a French medical doctor, François Quesnay, who utilized the physiology of blood flows in the human body to provide an interpretation of the economy as a set of flows!

<u>Note</u>: as we study the macroeconomy, we operate with an analytical distinction between a *closed* and an *open* economy. A closed economy is assumed to have no economic interactions with the rest of the world and is typically used to introduce students to fundamental macroeconomic variables and relationships. An open economy is a much more realistic, and analytically much more complex, representation of our economies. In this introductory course we'll concern ourselves mostly with a closed economy.

Fundamental macroeconomic identities

In order to approach an economy as a set of flows, we need to introduce some fundamental macroeconomic identities first; and given that we are now interested in the study of an economy as *aggregate economic activity*, we need to first establish ways in which such aggregate economic activity can be measured. The so-called *Product Approach, Income Approach,* and *Expenditure Approach* come to our rescue by giving us identical <u>measurements of aggregate economic activity</u>:

- the <u>*Product Approach*</u> gives a measurement of overall economic activity by looking at the value of what is produced within a certain period of time;
- the <u>*Income Approach*</u> gives a measurement of economic activity by looking at the income received by the owners (households) of the factors of production (labor, capital, land) used in the same period of time;
- the <u>*Expenditure Approach*</u> gives a measurement of aggregate economic activity by looking at the total value of all spending by all economic agents on goods/services in the same period of time.

As noted earlier, these three approaches give us identical quantitative measurements of the aggregate economic activity of a country in a given period of time, *but why do they?* Intuitively, the reason is actually quite straightforward and relies on the <u>concept of value</u>: the value of the production of goods/services is by definition equal to the sum of the costs of production and profits paid out by all the firms. These costs of production and profits, seen from the perspective of the receivers of the firms' payments, are the income received by the owners of all the factors of production, and these owners of the factors of production are the economy's households. Thus, the value of aggregate production must be equal to the value of aggregate income. The income received by the households can only be spent, either directly (direct purchase of goods/services) or indirectly, by placing it in savings accounts that are then used by banks to lend to firms and possibly the government for their purchase of goods and services. Thus, the value of aggregate income must also be equal to the value of total expenditure.

So, we can write:

$$TOTAL\ PRODUCTION = TOTAL\ INCOME = TOTAL\ EXPENDITURE$$

$$Y = wages + rents + interests + profits = C + I + G + NX \tag{5.1}$$

where:

Y   Aggregate output, or aggregate income;
C   Consumption: purchases of goods and services by households;
I   Investments: purchases of (capital) goods by firms;
G   Public expenditure: purchases of goods and services by the public sector (government);
NX   Net exports: purchases of domestic goods and services by foreigners (exports), net of domestic purchases of foreign goods and services (imports).

These fundamental identities become more intuitive as we consider the economy as a system of flows of products, income, and expenditure.

Circular flows within an economy

Let's see how flows can characterize a macroeconomy, beginning with the simplest way we can think of an economy: one consisting only of households, firms, and financial institutions (case a), and then gradually approach more complex (and realistic) cases by adding the government (case b) and the rest of the world (case c).

Case a: Simplest case – closed economy without public sector

FIGURE 5.1   Flow diagram of closed economy, no public sector

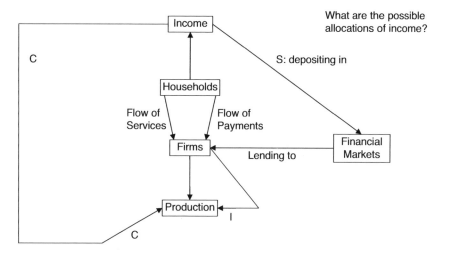

Thus, our fundamental identity in this case is:

TOTAL EXPENDITURES ON PRODUCTION = TOTAL ALLOCATION OF INCOME

$$C + I = C + S \qquad\qquad (5.2)$$

where S indicates "savings."

When the economy is in equilibrium (consumption goods and services *purchased* equals to consumption goods and services *produced*), this identity implies the following equality:

$S = I$: <u>National Savings equals Investments</u>: this is the *macroeconomic equilibrium condition of a closed economy without public sector*.

<u>Note</u>: The terms *savings* and *investment* may be confusing, as lay people tend to use them interchangeably. In macroeconomics, <u>investments</u> have a very precise and distinctive meaning: *investments are only the purchases of new capital goods, such as equipment and buildings, by firms*. In the language of macroeconomics, if you say that someone "*invests* in a treasury bond," this someone does not actually *invest*: they *save*.

Case b: One degree more realistic – closed economy with public sector

FIGURE 5.2   Flow diagram of closed economy with public sector

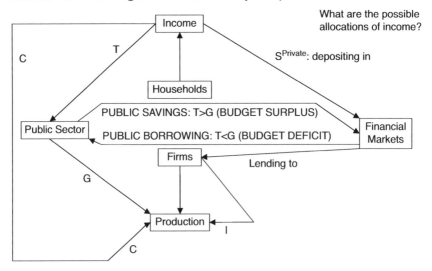

The fundamental identity in this case is:

TOTAL EXPENDITURES ON PRODUCTION = TOTAL ALLOCATION OF INCOME

$$C + G + I = C + S^{Private} + T \qquad (5.3)$$

where T indicates Taxes, G indicates Government expenditure, and $S^{Private}$ indicates savings by households.

The *macroeconomic equilibrium condition of a closed economy with a public sector* then is given by:

$$S^{Private} - I = G - T \qquad (5.4)$$

Recall also that if $T > G$, then the government is running a *budget surplus*, and this surplus is equal to *"public savings."* So, the equilibrium condition can be also written as:

$$S^{Private} + (T - G) = S^{Private} + S^{Public} = I \qquad (5.5)$$

■ ■ ■

Opportunities for further reflection

- Notice that: if $S^{Private} > I$, then the economy must be running a budget deficit $(G > T)$. Why could that be? What sort of intuition do you have about this relationship?
- What happens to investments when public expenditure is increased without a corresponding increase in taxes, *ceteris paribus*?

■ ■ ■

Case c: Open economy

Let goods and services cross borders. Then, building on the last flow diagram, we add another possible source of expenditure on domestic goods (goods purchased by foreigners, i.e. <u>exports</u>) and another possible allocation of income (domestic consumption of foreign goods, i.e. <u>imports</u>). So, the fundamental identity in this case is:

TOTAL EXPENDITURES ON PRODUCTION = TOTAL ALLOCATION OF INCOME

$$C + G + I + X = C + S^{Private} + T + M \tag{5.6}$$

where X indicates exports, and M indicates imports.

When the economy is in equilibrium, this identity implies the following equality:

$$S^{Private} - I = (G - T) + (X - M) \tag{5.7}$$
excess of domestic (private) savings = budget deficit + trade surplus

The *microeconomic equilibrium condition of an open economy with public sector* is then given by:

$$S^{Private} = I + (G - T) + (X - M) \tag{5.8}$$

This is a tricky equation! It makes sense that private savings have to feed the budget deficit (borrowing of funds by the government) and investments (borrowing of funds by firms), but why should private savings (also) finance the trade surplus?

The idea is that if the economy runs a trade surplus, i.e., if it exports more than it imports, then it sells abroad more than it buys from abroad and ends up with a credit against the foreign country. In order to be paid, the country needs to "export" to the foreign country an equivalent amount of funds. This outflow of domestic funds is called _capital outflow_, and consists of the purchase of stocks, land, treasury bonds, etc., of the foreign country. In order to be able to do so, there has to be a domestic excess savings over domestic needs.

It is perhaps more intuitive to think of this relation in terms of currencies: if the US has a trade surplus with Brazil, it must give Brazil the amount of dollars needed in order for Brazil to pay for the extra imports (over exports) it has with the US. This boils down to financing the trade deficit that Brazil has with the US, or, equivalently, the trade surplus that the US has with Brazil. There is a close relation between high savings and trade surplus (e.g. China) and low savings and trade deficit (e.g. US).

Trade surplus and net capital outflow are therefore two sides of the same coin:

$$S^{Private} - I - (G - T) = NX \tag{5.9}$$

that is,

if > 0: net capital outflow (excess savings) « > 0: trade surplus
if < 0: net capital inflow (neg. net c. outflow) « < 0: trade deficit.

▓ 5.2 Macroeconomic goals and national income accounting

Macroeconomic theory provides the conceptual frameworks that allow poli-cymakers to identify and implement *appropriate* economic policies, and the *appropriateness* of any economic policy has to do with its ability to efficiently pursue the established objective. In general, macroeconomic policy is geared towards the fulfillment of at least one of the following three fundamental macroeconomic goals: *growth of the economy, price stability,* and *containment of unemployment.*

■ ■ ■

Opportunity for further reflection/discussion

Let's try to justify this list of goals:

- Economic growth, that is, the expansion of the *size* of the economy: why should this be a goal for a country? Are there reasons for which economies are better off if they grow in size? What are the drawbacks? (Note: these questions are discussed further in Chapter 8.)
- Price stability: keeping an eye on the rate at which prices increase or decrease. Why would it be a problem to have all prices, or their average of sorts, increase or decrease? Think about the effects of increasing (or decreasing) prices on lenders and borrowers: would both categories of people be equally affected? How about people that receive a fixed income? How about firms? Can you think of this issue internationally?
- Reducing unemployment: a pretty obvious goal, but should the government really do something about it? Wouldn't people find a job if they really wanted to? Should the government care?

■ ■ ■

First macroeconomic goal: enhance economic growth

If one has a goal, one has to have some variable able to give a sense of measurement that relates to the goal. If your goal is to finish the homework within a certain amount of time, a measurement of time is necessary. So, when we think of "economic growth," what are we measuring? We need a measure of the *size* of the economy, and such measure is provided by two fundamental concepts of national income accounting you have probably already heard of a million times:

Gross Domestic Product (*GDP*): market value of all the final goods/services produced in a given period of time (usually the calendar year) within national borders.

Gross National Product (*GNP*): market value of all the final goods/services produced in a given period of time (usually the calendar year) by domestically owned factors of production.

Note: *domestic* (the "D" in G<u>D</u>P) is linked to the concept of <u>borders,</u> and thus includes production by domestic and foreign firms within the borders of the country; and *national* (the "N" in G<u>N</u>P) is linked to the concept of <u>nationality</u> of factors of production, and thus includes production performed only by domestic firms, independently of whether such production occurs within or outside national borders.

Two key parts of these definitions require careful examination:

a.   <u>Final Goods and Services</u>
b.   <u>Market Value</u>

a. Final goods and services: the concept of value added

Not all goods and services produced in an economy are "final." Goods and services produced can be of two types:

- <u>intermediate</u>: goods and services that enter the production process of other goods and services; for instance, steel does not reach consumption directly, but enters other production processes in order to reach final consumers (e.g., appliances, cars, etc.).
- <u>final</u>: goods and services which are directly consumed, that is, goods and services that are bought as they are for final consumption.

It all sounds pretty straightforward, but … not so fast! Are the physical characteristics of a good or service sufficient to determine whether it is to be considered an intermediate or final one, and thus not enter or enter the calculation of GDP (or GNP)? According to the above definitions, would a "loaf of bread" be an intermediate or final good? Bread is certainly bought as is by consumers, but what if bread is sold as part of a restaurant's meal? And how would you categorize "banking services"? Sugar? Transportation services? And on and on.

As you can see, the distinction between final and intermediate goods and services is sometimes very tricky, because most goods and services are not categorizable as intermediate or final by their own physical characteristics. For steel, it's easy: it's not a consumption good by its own characteristic, i.e. it needs to be transformed further in order to reach households. But most goods and services are to be considered intermediate or final ones <u>depending on who buys them and for what</u>: if they are bought by a firm (that is, if they enter some further production process) they must be considered intermediate goods/services; if they are bought by final consumers, they must be considered final goods/services.

Why should we stress so much this distinction? Because only the market value of final goods and services enters the calculation of GDP: if we do not distinguish intermediate from final goods and services, we end up <u>double- or triple-counting or n-counting</u> them, as the value of intermediate goods is also included in the value of the final goods/services which use them in their production process. An example should clarify: think again about a loaf of bread and suppose it costs $1 to the final consumer. Thus, the contribution of the loaf of bread to GDP should be its value: $1. However, the price of the loaf of bread includes the compensation for flour, for the baker's service, and for the grocer's service: if we count each step of the production of the loaf of bread, we end up including in GDP a number much larger than $1. Suppose the following scenario, in which we don't distinguish between intermediate and final goods/services:

*the baker pays to the farmer (value of the flour):	$.3
*the grocer pays to the baker (value of flour & baker's service):	$.5
*the consumer pays to the grocer (value of flour, baker's service, & grocer's service):	$1
	--------
this number counts three times the service of the farmer, and twice the service of the baker!	$1.8

If we want to avoid this problem, i.e., avoid a gross overestimation of GDP, without having to go through the difficult judgment of which good/service is really final and which one is not, we can just keep track of what each activity adds to the value of the good/service, so bypassing the tricky distinction between final and intermediate goods. The concept of _value added_ helps us greatly here. <u>_Value added_ is the incremental increase in value of a good/service at each stage of the production process</u>. Continuing with the above example:

*the value added by the farmer (what (s)he's paid minus what (s)he pays, i.e. 0)	$.3
*the value added by the baker (what (s)he's paid minus what (s)he pays)	$.2
*the value added by the grocer (what (s)he's paid minus what (s)he pays)	$.5

	$1

Thus, by calculating the value added in each step of the production process we end up avoiding double- and triple-counting and n-counting, and, in fact, include in GDP only the value of goods and services at their final stage.

An important limitation of GDP and GNP is that some goods and services are not transacted in a market, do not have a market value, and thus end up excluded from the measurement. Examples include:

- education, defense: not having a price, they are computed at their costs;
- left-out activities: for instance, housework and child-rearing;
- non-declared activities: for tax purposes, or because illegal.
- ecological and environmental effects

Also, be aware that different levels of development across countries can affect the percentage of economic activity properly accounted for. Pure comparisons of GDP across countries at very different levels of development can therefore be misleading. Another problematic aspect of GDP becomes particularly relevant when GDP is used in *per capita* terms (GDP/population) to evaluate and compare standards of living across countries. For instance, in 2016 Qatar had an *income per capita* (GDP *per capita*) which was three times higher than the income per capita of Denmark, but would you feel comfortable concluding that the *average* standard of living in Qatar is three times higher than the average standard of living in Denmark?

b. Market value: concepts of Nominal GDP and Real GDP

The second focus point of our definition of GDP was the *market value* of goods and services. Market value means that the goods and services are evaluated at market prices.

But which prices? Prices of any year? Of the same year in which we calculate GDP? Of a different year? Depending on whether we choose to use prices of the current year (the same year in which we are measuring the aggregate economic activity) or prices of an established, fixed year, we obtain, respectively, *nominal* GDP and *real* GDP.

- If we calculate GDP at *current prices*, i.e., at prices prevailing in the same year for which we are computing the GDP, we get what is known as *nominal GDP*.
- If we calculate GDP at *constant prices*, i.e., at prices prevailing in a year chosen to be the *base year*, we get what is known as *real GDP*.

The most important difference between the two definitions is that while a variation of real GDP between two different years reflects only the variation of the quantities produced (as the prices at which production is evaluated remain constant); a variation of nominal GDP between two different years may reflect not only the difference in the quantities actually produced, but also of the prices at which those quantities have been evaluated.

Important! Whenever we want to know whether an economy has grown and at what rate, we use *real GDP*; whenever we want to know whether the average standard of living of an economy has grown and at what rate, we use *real GDP per capita*.

So, to measure the rate of growth of the economy, say, between 2015 and 2016, assuming the base year is 2012, we calculate:

$$\%\Delta GDP_{Real} = \frac{GDP_{Real}^{2016} - GDP_{Real}^{2015}}{GDP_{Real}^{2015}} \times 100$$

$$= \frac{GDP_{b.y.2012}^{2016} - GDP_{b.y.2012}^{2015}}{GDP_{b.y.2012}^{2015}} \times 100 \tag{5.10}$$

Note: Why do we need prices at all to evaluate the *size* of an economy? We are interested in the size of aggregate economic activity, and we need to be able to compare it over years and across countries. If we do not make use of prices, what would we say if, for instance, in one year the economy produces 10,000 cars and 20,000 bicycles, and the year after it produces 5,000 cars and 25,000 bicycles? Did the economy produce more in the first or second year? Prices allow us to overcome this indeterminacy.

■ ■ ■

Opportunity for further reflection

Suppose that we choose 1930 as the base year and use it to calculate and then compare a long series of real GDPs, say, from 1930 to 2015. Can you foresee any difficulty in doing this? Or, say, suppose that we choose

1960 as the base year to do the same thing: again, can you foresee any difficulty in doing this?

■ ■ ■

Second macroeconomic goal: price stability

Again, if we have a goal, we have to have a way of measuring how we are doing relative to the goal. In this case, the measurement of the variability of prices through time is given by the *inflation rate*, defined as the percentage increase in the *general level of prices* in a given period of time (like a month, a quarter, or a year). We say we have *deflation* if the general level of prices decreases over a given period of time.

The difficulty with measuring inflation should be relatively straightforward: if all prices (prices of all goods and services) go up together by the same percentage, measuring inflation would be very easy. It would just be the percentage increase of "all" prices. Unfortunately, this is not what typically happens in reality. For instance, in the past 30 years, the price of vegetables has increased by 220 percent and the price of gasoline by 140 percent, while the price of computers has declined by 90 percent. So, what to say about the "overall" change in prices?

Economists get around this problem by calculating "indexes," that is, weighted-averages of all price changes. The most common index for inflation is the Consumer Price Index.

The *Consumer Price Index* (CPI) is a fixed-weight index that compares the value of a fixed basket of goods and services representative of the consumption pattern of the average *urban* consumer in two different time periods (the Bureau of Labor Statistics of the US Department of Labor, for instance, calculates this index monthly):

$$CPI = \frac{\text{value of a fixed basket of consumer goods at current prices}}{\text{value of the same basket at base year prices}} \quad (5.11)$$

EXAMPLE

Consider the following basket of goods: 50% oranges (O), 50% potatoes (P), and assume the following prices:

$$P_{O,\,1990} = \$.25; P_{P,\,1990} = \$.05; P_{O,\,1991} = \$.30; P_{P,\,1991}$$

$$= \$.05; \text{base year: } 1990$$

$$CPI_{1990} = 1$$

$$CPI_{1991} = [.5\,(.30) + .5\,(.05)] / [.5\,(.25) + .5\,(.05)] = 1.16$$

$\%\Delta CPI = 16\%$: in 1991 this basket of goods had a price value that was 1.16 times its price value in 1990. Thus, the 1991 inflation rate, as measured by the CPI, was 16%.

Third macroeconomic goal: contain unemployment

According to the Bureau of Labor Statistics, data on population and employment in the US, as of June 2019, was as follows:

Population	329,224,000	
Civilian Working Age Population	259,037,000	
Not in the Labor Force	96,056,000	
Labor Force	162,981,000	(62.9% of Working Age Population)
Employed	157,005,000	
(Involuntary) Unemployed	5,975,000	

where:

- Civilian Working Age Population: Total population *minus* people who by law cannot work (<16, institutionalized) and those in the military;
- Labor Force: Working Age Population *minus* people who are not active in the labor market ("Not in the labor force," that is, without a job and not looking for a job: voluntary unemployment);
- Involuntary Unemployment (unemployment proper): Labor Force *minus* Employed People.

Given this data, macroeconomists derive important statistics that measure how well the labor market performs:

$$Unemployment\ Rate = \frac{\#\ of\ Unemployed\ People}{\#\ in\ the\ Labor\ Force} \times 100 \qquad (5.12)$$

$$Labor\ Force\ Participation\ Rate = \frac{\#\ in\ the\ Labor\ Force}{\#\ in\ Working\ Age\ Population} \times 100 \quad (5.13)$$

$$Employment\ to\ Population\ Rate = \frac{\#\ Employed}{\#\ in\ Working\ Age\ Population} \times 100 \quad (5.14)$$

In June 2019, the values of these statistics in the US were:

Unemployment Rate	3.7%
Labor Force Participation Rate	62.9%
Employment-to-Population Rate	60.6%

As you are probably very well aware, the most followed statistic of the labor market is the *unemployment rate*. Verbally, we define it as <u>the percentage of people who are active in the labor force and do not have a job, relative to the total number of people in the labor force</u>.

A number of economic phenomena affect the rate of unemployment of a country. A categorization of the main causes of unemployment gives rise to the following sub-definitions:

- *Frictional unemployment*: unemployment due to the time workers spend in job search. A certain amount of frictional unemployment is inevitable, as there is always a certain number of workers between jobs.
- *Structural unemployment*: permanent displacement of workers due to shifts in demand of products, technological change, international competition, international outsourcing, and so on (e.g.: the decline of manufacturing jobs in the US).
- *Cyclical unemployment*: unemployment due to the decreased demand for labor during recessions.
- *Hidden unemployment*: many people would like a job if they thought one was available but become discouraged and remain outside the labor force. Thus, they are not counted as *involuntarily* unemployed, even though they actually are (they are also known as *discouraged workers*).
- *Seasonal unemployment*: seasonal changes in demand and supply of labor.[1]

▨ 5.3 Business cycles and trend

Recall the Production Possibility Frontier discussed in Chapter 2, which gives us the combinations of (maximum) output of two goods or services when the available resources are fully employed and efficiently used. Imagine that we apply the same idea to the whole economy. You would not be able to draw this Production Possibility Frontier, as the whole economy consists of millions of goods and services, but the concept remains the same: <u>when the whole economy employs the available resources (labor and capital, i.e., machines) fully and efficiently, the output produced would be at the economy's *potential*</u>.

We call this "ideal" level of output: *full employment level of output*, or *potential level of output*, or *capacity level of output*. They are all synonyms.

If we calculate the potential (real) GDP of the economy year after year, we are likely to obtain an increasing number: the economy's PPF expands every year (as population increases, capital accumulates, technology improves, and so on), and so does the *full employment level of output*. If we plot the *full employment levels of output* against time, as in Figure 5.3, we should therefore obtain an upward sloping line that we call the <u>trend</u> of the economy.

Yet, when we look at historical real GDP data, i.e. the actual values of the economy's real GDP year after year, we immediately notice that the economy is very rarely at potential; it actually fluctuates around its *trend* in very irregular patterns. The economy's fluctuations around the trend are referred to as the <u>business cycle</u> of the economy (the name is somewhat misleading, as the term "cycle" gives a sense of regularity, but there is no historical regularity in these cycles).

FIGURE 5.3   Business cycle and long-run trend in the economy

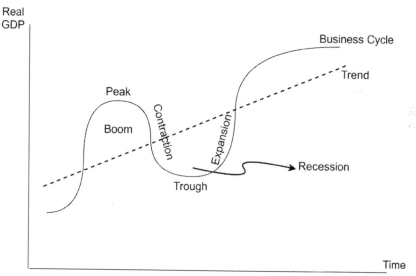

Strong upward fluctuations are called <u>booms</u>, and downward ones are called <u>recessions</u> or <u>contractions</u>. Severe downturns are referred to as <u>depressions</u>. The last depression in the US and many other countries, called the Great Depression because of its length and depth, began in 1929, and the economy did not fully recover from it until World War II. While there is no technical definition of a boom, <u>a recession is said to have occurred when real</u>

GDP falls for at least two consecutive quarters. The bottom of a recession is called *trough*, and the top of a boom is called *peak*. The economy *expands* from trough to peak, and *contracts* from peak to trough.

The business cycle of an economy is therefore a sequence of recessions and booms.

- In a recession, the economy operates *below potential*, that is, *below full employment*. The most important economic problem during a recession is then <u>unemployment</u>. Thus, during a recession the main goal of macroeconomic policy is typically the reduction of unemployment.
- In a boom, the economy operates *above potential*, that is, *above full employment*. Here, the most important economic problem is the "overheating" of the economy: demand for resources exceeds supply, typically causing prices to increase too rapidly. Thus, during a boom, the main goal of macroeconomic policy is typically the containment of inflation.

■ ■ ■

Opportunity for further reflection

How can the economy ever operate *above full employment*? Can you think of examples?

■ ■ ■

5.4 What else should count? Measuring time use

While measuring factors like GDP (and GDP per-capita) and its components, unemployment, and inflation is the traditional focus of national income accounting, feminist economists have long argued that important aspects of economic activity are left out of this framework.[2] Note that these macroeconomic measurements focus exclusively on work and economic activity that takes place in markets. As discussed in section 5.2 of this chapter, GDP leaves out many things, such as unpaid housework and childcare. These things are, no doubt, economic activity – after all, many of them can be moved to the marketplace. Imagine that you go to a restaurant to have a meal. Your payment for the meal is added to GDP. That includes the value added in growing and processing all of the ingredients for your meal, food preparation, serving the food, and cleaning up. However, if you purchase food from the grocery store and prepare it at home, only the value of the ingredients is added to GDP. Either way, you have a meal, but, when you have it at home, much of the economic activity is not counted in GDP.

Extensive work has been undertaken by feminist economists and those in other economic subfields (such as ecological economics) to estimate the activity and value in sectors left out of GDP. In addition to trying to understand the value of these economic activities in money terms, though, feminist economists have pioneered surveys that seek to understand how people use their *time*. As a result, time use surveys are now conducted in most countries in the world. In the US, the American Time Use Survey (ATUS) is released every year. It can help economists understand how people use their time differently, highlighting inequalities between different groups of people, and, especially between men and women. Differences in the use of time (and the expectations of how time *should* be used – that is, who should be responsible for what in a household) can shape many market outcomes. For example, if women are expected to clean a home and take care of children *in addition to* working for pay in the market, while men do not face these expectations, we would expect to see differences in the types of jobs that women take (this is discussed much more in Chapter 8). Note, too, that people who are not living with a partner or those living with a partner of the same sex will display different time-use patterns (with different impacts on their economic choices!).

Table 5.1 shows some interesting results from the American Time Use Survey from 2007 and 2017 for men and women. Here, "household activities" refer to things like cleaning, laundry, food preparation and cleanup, lawn and garden care, home maintenance, and taking care of pets. Note

TABLE 5.1 American Time Use Survey selected results

Indicator	2007 Survey		2017 Survey	
	MEN	WOMEN	MEN	WOMEN
% doing household activities	65.6	82.7	68.0	84.0
Avg time on household activities	1.43h	2.22h	1.41h	2.19h
% caring for and helping household members	20.3	30.4	20.0	29.0
Avg time on care (of those doing it)	1.62h	2.38h	1.79h	2.34h
Avg leisure time	5.71h	4.98h	5.53h	4.98h
Avg time working and work-related activities for pay (of those working)	8.34h	7.53h	8.66h	7.67h

Source: US Bureau of Labor Statistics

that, in both years, more women perform these kinds of tasks than men, and women spend much more time on them in an average day (more than 45 minutes!). Women also spend more time caring for household members, have less leisure time and spend less time working for pay. The survey results show some deep inequalities in how people spend their time in the US, and this changes only slightly in the 10 years between the results presented here.

■ ■ ■

Opportunity for further reflection

Why do you think social norms attached to gender are so persistent? How might such inequalities be remedied through policies? What might be the limits of such policies?

■ ■ ■

Notes

1. Most unemployment figures that you see are "seasonally adjusted" to remove this component of unemployment. Economists agree that this kind of unemployment is less relevant for understanding the state of the macroeconomy, though there could be cases where understanding the seasonal fluctuations in employment can be useful.
2. As you may recall in Chapter 1, this was first written about extensively by Marilyn Waring in her book *If Women Counted: A New Feminist Economics* (1989).

6

In the short run we are alive

Macroeconomic theory and policy: the goods market

6.1 Introduction to the Classical – or *supply-side* – theoretical framework

Depending on how efficient you believe markets are, you may consider the cyclical fluctuations around the trend as transitory phenomena that will be directly and relatively quickly eliminated by the market mechanism itself; or you may consider them as sub-optimal situations in which the economy can get stuck for a relatively long time below potential, and potentially never recover from it without external help. These two "belief systems" distinguish the two most important macroeconomic paradigms: the Classical and the Keynesian. These two paradigms are also often referred to as the <u>long-run macroeconomic model</u> and the <u>short-run macroeconomic model</u>, with the idea that *in the long-run* the economy would in fact be operating at capacity level (on the trend), and so the Classical model would be the more appropriate one to use when one thinks in long-run terms. But as Keynes said ... in the long-run we'll all be dead, so ... act in the short run!

The Classical paradigm refers to the very first modern school of economic thought: *Classical Political Economy*, which enjoyed substantial popularity in England from the end of the Napoleonic Wars (1815) to the 1850s. Classical political economists thought about the macroeconomy as a plain aggregation of markets: only intellectual tools typical of microeconomics were used to analyze the overall economy (later on, in the second half of the twentieth century, this approach to macroeconomics became known as *micro-founded*; its main scholarly home is in the department of economics of the University of Chicago, and that is why in the late 1970s the Classical approach became also known as *freshwater* – as opposed to *saltwater* – macroeconomics).

The Classical macroeconomic paradigm concludes that the economy is completely self-adjusting because of the following two assumptions.

- <u>Markets work quickly, flexibly, and efficiently</u>: if there is an excess supply or an excess demand of any good, service or resource, prices adjust immediately and effectively so that the equilibrium is automatically reached.
- <u>Supply creates its own demand</u>: this is known as *Say's Law*, already encountered in Chapter 1, an idea introduced by the Classical economist Jean Baptiste Say in his 1803 *Treatise of Political Economy*. According to this law, an increase in production automatically causes the increase in demand necessary to purchase the additional output. This is because an increase in production causes an equal increase in income, and income, as we have learned, can only be spent (directly or indirectly). This view is represented in Figure 5.1 in Chapter 5. An obvious critique to this law would say that even if income increases by the same amount as production, this additional income does not need to be spent on the additional goods that have been produced. Say considered this critique and replied that mismatches between additional supply and additional demand can only happen because entrepreneurs erroneously increased the supply of goods that are not in demand: given that this is the last thing entrepreneurs want, they will correct their own mistakes until in fact additional supply and additional demand are equal.

The combination of these two fundamental points leads to the main conclusion of the Classical framework: <u>*output (or income) can only be at full employment!* Any deviation from *full employment* has to be transitory, short-lived, and therefore best dealt with by letting the markets do their job, i.e., self-adjust quickly and effectively.</u>

■ ■ ■

Opportunity for further reflection

Suppose that population, and thus the labor force, increases. The economy would immediately experience an excess supply of labor, i.e., involuntary unemployment. How would a Classical economist see the economy readjusting to full employment?

■ ■ ■

Consequently, from a policy point of view, a Classical macroeconomist would never want to intervene in the real side of the economy, as intervening in the economy would only have the effect of slowing down and potentially messing up the otherwise perfectly functioning market mechanism. This particular approach to policy (actually, *non* policy) is known as *laissez faire*, and today it characterizes a conservative approach to economic policy. Not so when it was introduced in the eighteenth century! At that time, the conservative view of the economy was in fact interventionist (mercantilism), with the objective to maintain the economic and political power in the hands of the aristocracy and the already wealthy merchants. Classical political economists stood for the elimination of government interventions in the economy as a way to eliminate the privileges of the aristocracy and to spread well-being across the whole population. Thus, originally the *laissez faire* approach to economic policy was truly progressive – very much the opposite of how it is today, with its strongly anti-redistributive rhetoric.

The Classical, *supply-side* approach monopolized macroeconomic studies until the Great Depression, when it proved unable to explain the continuing, long-term deterioration of the economy, and thus unable to provide any effective policy remedy. The Classical approach was then superseded by the Keynesian framework, formally introduced by John Maynard Keynes in 1936 with the publication of his *The General Theory of Employment, Interest, and Money.*

6.2 Classical framework – The Loanable Funds Model: determination of the interest rate in the real side of the economy

As seen earlier, the Classical assumptions of efficient markets and Say's Law lead to the conclusion that <u>output (or income) is always at full employment</u>. In the previous chapter we introduced the symbol for output (or income): Y. To indicate that the level of output is always at full employment, we place a "bar" on top of Y: so $\bar{Y}$ means "full-employment output" (or "full-employment income").

In order to study the Classical equilibrium conditions in the *goods market* (the *real* side of the economy), let's assume that our economy is closed (no trade with the rest of the world) and with public sector (case b of the flow diagrams discussed in Chapter 5). You may recall that the macroeconomic equilibrium condition in this case is:

$$S^{Pr} + (T - G) = I \tag{6.1}$$

where (T–G) is equal to *Public Savings* (S^{Pu}). Substituting, and indicating the sum of Private and Public Savings with S^N (as "National Savings"):

$$S^{Pr} + S^{Pu} = S^N \tag{6.2}$$

the macroeconomic equilibrium condition can be rewritten as:

$$S^N = I \qquad \qquad (6.3)$$

Let's see what characterizes these different variables.

- T and G are considered variables determined through the country's political process; we look up the budget decisions of Congress, and take their numbers for T and G as given. This implies that, for us, S^{Pu} is a given number. As an example, suppose we find out from Congress that: $T = 1,000$ and $G = 800$. This implies that our $S^{Pu} = 200$.
- S^{Pr} symbolizes savings by households. Remember the "story" behind the flow diagrams: households receive income, $\bar{Y}$, and use it for Taxes, Consumption, and (Private) Savings. Once Taxes are paid, the remainder $(\bar{Y} - T)$, known as *disposable income*, is fully allocated to consumption and savings. The simplest way we can model the allocation of disposable income by households is to think that fixed (and known) percentages of disposable income are allocated to consumption and savings. Thus, because $\bar{Y}$ is known and fixed, and Taxes are determined by the political process, also S^{Pr} turns out to be a given number.

  E.g. Assume that $\bar{Y} = 5,000$, and that households save 20% of their disposable income. We saw earlier that T = 1,000. Then:
  Disposable income = $(\bar{Y} - T) = 5,000 - 1,000 = 4,000$
  Private Savings = $S^{Pr} = .2(\bar{Y} - T) = .2 (4,000) = 800$

- Investments (I) are decisions to purchase new capital goods by firms. What determines the level of investments firms may want to undertake? Recall again the flow chart: firms borrow funds from banks in order to purchase capital goods; the cost of borrowing funds is the interest rate banks charge: the higher the interest rate is, the higher the cost of borrowing funds is; and the higher the cost of borrowing funds is, the smaller the pool of profitable investments is. Thus, investments turn out to have an inverse relationship with the interest rate: the higher the interest rate is, the less firms tend to invest (the lower the level of investments is). We write:

  $I = I(r)$ and read it as: "Investments are a (negative) function of the interest rate;"
  "r" indicates the real interest rate paid by firms to borrow funds from banks.

E.g., Suppose that the investment function is $I = -100r + 2,000$
Investments are represented by a negatively sloped line ("r"
on the vertical axis); when $r = 0$, $I = 2,000$; when $r = 20$,
$I = 0$.

We now have all the components that are necessary to look at the macroeconomic equilibrium of this economy; using the numerical examples given
above:

$$S^{Pr} = 800$$
$$S^{Pu} = 200$$
$$I = -100r + 2,000$$

we can now directly substitute them in the equilibrium condition:

$$S^{Pr} + S^{Pu} = I$$
$$800 + 200 = -100r + 2,000$$
$$100r = 1,000$$
$$r^* = 10$$

The macroeconomic equilibrium condition for this economy, according to
the Classical framework (output at full employment) is: the interest rate "r"
has to be equal to 10. When the interest rate is equal to 10, the amount of
funds firms want to borrow is exactly equal to the amount of funds banks
collect through private and public savings (in our example, this amount of
funds is: 1,000):

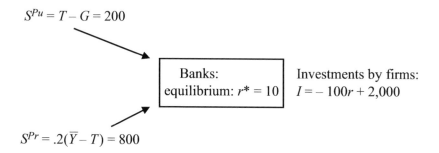

$S^{Pu} = T - G = 200$

Banks:
equilibrium: $r^* = 10$

Investments by firms:
$I = -100r + 2,000$

$S^{Pr} = .2(\overline{Y} - T) = 800$

In this Classical framework in which output is always at full employment,
the macroeconomic equilibrium boils down to the equilibrium between the
aggregate demand and aggregate supply of funds: that's why this approach to
equilibrium is known as the _Loanable Funds Model._

The graphical representation of our example is as follows:

FIGURE 6.1   Loanable Funds Model

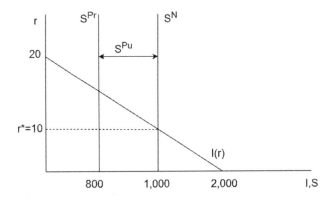

 ## 6.3 Macroeconomic policy in the Classical framework: goods market

An *economic policy* consists of the modification of one or more economic variables, with the objective of moving the resulting equilibrium in the desired direction. While Classical economists generally advocate for government's non-intervention, they often support certain types of policy.

Possible policies that can alter the *Loanable Funds Model* equilibrium are:

1. fiscal policy: change in Public Spending (G), and/or Taxation (T);
2. nudging firms to invest more, by infusing them with optimism about the future of the economy;
3. nudging households to save a different percentage of their disposable income.

What should the goal of macroeconomic policy be in the Classical framework? Recall the three goals of macroeconomic policy: enhance growth, maintain price stability, and contain unemployment. Given that this section only pertains to the *real* side of the economy, we should consider only the first and third goals. But then: is the third goal relevant in the Classical framework? Would a Classical economist utilize policy in order to contain unemployment? Can there be persistent unemployment in a Classical framework? The fundamental assumption of a Classical model is full employment! As said earlier, any deviation from full employment is considered transitory, and best taken care of by the market itself. So, <u>the only goal that macroeconomic policy should pursue in the *real* side of the economy is, enhance economic growth, that is, expand $\bar{Y}$</u>: make the trend steeper!

Let's recall what the full employment level of output $\bar{Y}$ depends on: the same variables that affect the position of the PPF. You may remember that the PPF expands when the available amount of resources increases (labor, capital, land, or natural resources), and/or there is technological improvement. So, in general, *desirable policies* in the Classical framework are policies that increase the capital stock of the economy (i.e., policies that induce firms to invest more), policies that support an increase in the labor force, and policies that support improvements in technology.

Let's then evaluate the three sets of policies listed above using the basic graph of the loanable funds model.

1.   Fiscal policy: effects of, say, an increase in G or a decrease in T (i.e., a reduction of the budget surplus or an increase in the budget deficit), shown in Figure 6.2.

FIGURE 6.2   Loanable Funds Model: effects of expansionary fiscal policy

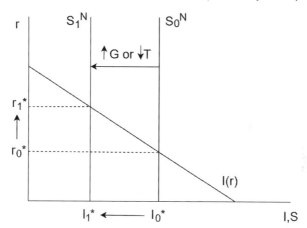

Such policy would decrease the amount of funds available for investments (National Savings, S^N, shifts leftward): the interest rate would rise, and the level of investments would decrease. This does not appear to be a desirable policy for a Classical macroeconomist: a decrease in investments decreases the rate of accumulation of capital and thus slows down economic growth.

■ ■ ■

Class discussion

We just saw that an increase in the budget deficit would decrease the level of investments and thus economic growth. Yet, we hear such proposals from the Republicans in Congress and Presidential Administrations: an increase in public spending ($1 trillion increase in infrastructure spending); a decrease in tax rates leading to a decrease in taxes; and so on. According to the Committee for Responsible Federal Budget, "President Trump's proposed changes to the tax code could increase the deficit by an estimated $3 trillion to $7 trillion over the next decade" (*The New York Times*, April 26, 2017). Does it make sense that a conservative government pushes for an increase in the budget deficit? What may we be missing by analyzing the effects of fiscal policy through the Loanable Funds Model?

■ ■ ■

2.   <u>Nudging firms</u> to invest more, by infusing them with optimism about the future of the economy.

This nudging policy, shown in Figure 6.3, is meant to make firms invest more, at any given interest rate: the investment function shifts to the right. Notice that in our simplified scenario National Savings do not depend on the interest rate, and thus, the supply of funds does not change as the interest rate changes. Thus, an increase in firms' willingness to invest results *only* in an increase in the interest rate without any actual impact on the level of investments (I^* remains constant). The interest rate increases because there is an excess demand of loanable funds caused by the firms' increased willingness to invest, while the supply of funds remains constant.

FIGURE 6.3   Loanable Funds Model: nudging firms to invest more

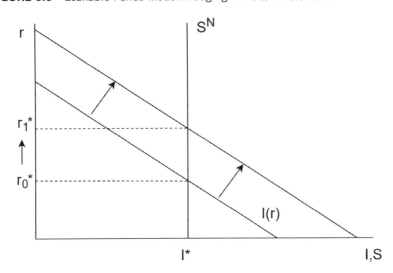

■ ■ ■

Opportunity for further reflection

In a more realistic scenario, in which Private Savings depend positively on the interest rate, would the overall effect of such *nudging* policy be different?

■ ■ ■

3. <u>Nudging households</u> to save a different percentage of their disposable income.

Suppose that some government agency is successful in convincing households to save a higher percentage of their disposable income. Private Savings would increase, and thus National Savings would increase, shown in Figure 6.4.

FIGURE 6.4   Loanable Funds Model: nudging households to save more

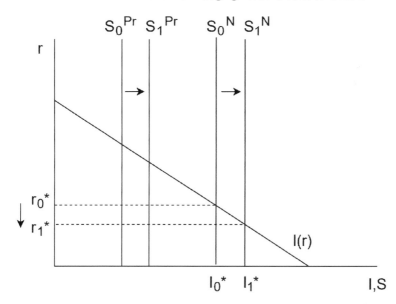

An increase in the supply of funds pushes the interest rate down. A lower interest rate increases the level of investments firms are willing to undertake. Given that the overall effect of this policy is an increase in investments, this is a very desirable outcome for a Classical macroeconomist.

■ ■ ■

Opportunity for further reflection

Oh wait! But if households save more out of their disposable income, who's going to buy the consumption goods firms will produce with the additional investments? What happens to Say's Law?

■ ■ ■

Let's recap the Classical framework. The Classical, *supply-side* model conceives the economy as always at full employment: every movement away from the full employment level of output (and therefore income) is quickly corrected by movements in prices, so that resources are always fully employed, and the supply of every good and service finds its own demand (Say's Law). The business cycle – the ups and downs of the economy – in the Classical framework is seen as completely transitory and self-correcting: the business of macroeconomists is to interfere the least with the *natural* movement of the economy along the trend. Macroeconomic equilibrium in this model is guaranteed by the interest rate, that adjusts so that the supply of funds in the economy (National Savings) is equal to the demand of funds (investments). This is why this model is also known as the *Loanable Funds Model*. In this model, the higher savings are, the higher investments are: investments are capital formation, and higher levels of capital expand the country's PPF, that is, increases the level of full employment output. As the level of output increases (economic growth), the trickle-down mechanism supposedly raises the standard of living of all classes of society (assuming perfect competition all around ... remember Adam Smith's story from Chapter 1?).

The grand failure of the Classical model: the Great Depression

This Classical model was the go-to model of macroeconomists for about 100 years. But then came the Great Depression, the market crash of 1929, and the disastrous years that followed: an economic and social disaster that spread around the globe from 1929 to 1939. The business cycle ceased to be self-correcting: the market mechanism failed again and again, and with it, the Classical model too.

Just to remind you of the gravity of this "failure" of markets to bring the economy back to full-employment, consider some of the most important economic facts of the Great Depression, at least in the US.[1]

- During the 1920s, the agricultural sector was deeply transformed by mechanization: there was an increase in agricultural output, but the drop in prices caused by the initial surplus failed to increase the quantity demanded; this, together with other reasons (such as the decrease in agricultural exports to Europe, which had rebounded after having decreased during WWI), produced a decrease in the number of independent farmers by 40 % within a decade.
- Even though manufacturing output was at an all-time high during the 1920s, towards the end of the decade many manufacturers began to anticipate an economic downturn and reduced their workforces substantially. A lopsided distribution of income, which had produced very high profits but no improvement in the workers' conditions, had created situations of surplus in many markets. Thus, even if profits at the end of the decade were three times as high as at the beginning of the 1920s, firms did not reinvest, as there were no incentives to increase supply.
- Mismanaged financially fragile banks had produced suspicions that if customers requested their deposits back, the banks would not be able to pay. This produced "runs" of customers asking for their money back, which produced the collapse of a large number of banks: about 7,000 US banks failed during the Great Depression (Federal Reserve).
- The US government followed a balanced budget philosophy, increasing taxes and decreasing public spending to reduce the budget deficit; by negatively affecting the aggregate demand of goods, it made the situation even worse.
- In 1930, the US passed the Smoot-Hawley tariff act, that imposed a 45% tariff on most imported goods, to try to switch demand from imported goods to domestic goods, and thus reduce domestic unemployment. But all it did was to cause retaliation, and the most famous recent trade war ensued: the volume of world trade decreased by about 66% between 1930 and 1934.

A few more numbers:

- Between 1929 and 1932: 85,000 US businesses failed, and the value of stocks decreased by 80%.
- Manufacturing and agricultural income decreased by 50%.
- Unemployment stood at about 25% (average).
- Aggregate prices declined on average by over 30%.
- Real GDP in 1929 was $104 billion; in 1933 it was $56 billion.

Clearly markets were not self-correcting! The economy was in fact moving further and further away from its full-employment equilibrium.

6.4 Introduction to the Keynesian theoretical framework

It was John Maynard Keynes, a British economist educated at Cambridge, that was the first to understand and formalize what was needed to get the economy out of the depression. His most important contribution, *The General Theory of Employment, Interest, and Money*, published in 1936, revolutionized economics. In fact, according to many economists, *de facto* it began the field of macroeconomics.

Keynes introduced two fundamental ideas that changed the way the macroeconomy and macroeconomic policy were conceived:

1. <u>Output can be persistently different from its full employment level</u>: it is not that the supply creates its own demand, but the other way around. Thus, he discarded Say's Law. This has the important consequence that it is the aggregate demand of the whole economy that determines the equilibrium level of output (or income).
2. <u>The interest rate</u> is not determined in the goods market: it <u>is a monetary variable</u>. In the next chapter we will see that this modification will allow for a much more effective role for monetary authorities (central banks) in the economy.

So, let's see how we can build a Keynesian macroeconomic model.

6.5 The *Keynesian Cross*: determination of equilibrium income (or output)

Recall the closed-economy fundamental identity between *product approach* (*output*, i.e., Y) and *expenditure approach* (i.e. sum of the expenditures by households, government, and firms) discussed in Chapter 5. In the Keynesian framework, where output can be persistently different from its full-employment level, it is the level of aggregate expenditure that determines the level of output. Thus:

Output = Aggregate Expenditure (AE)

$$Y = AE, \text{ i.e.,} \qquad (6.4)$$

$$Y = C + I + G \qquad (6.5)$$

Notice that here Y is not capped by a bar. Does that make sense to you? Can you see why?

Let's consider once again the components of Aggregate Expenditure one by one:

- We continue to consider <u>public spending</u> (G) and <u>taxation</u> (T) as "political" variables, whose values we obtain from Congress and take as given.
- We also continue to use the same form of <u>investment function</u>: $I = I(r)$ used before. Investments continue to be negatively related to the interest rate.
- We'll give, however, a bit more structure to the <u>consumption function</u>, by introducing the concepts of:
  - *Marginal propensity to consume* (mpc), which is the amount by which consumption rises if current disposable income increases by \$1: $mpc = \dfrac{\Delta C}{\Delta Y}$; and
  - *Autonomous consumption* (a), which is the amount of consumption spending a household would do if it had zero disposable income.

Notice that:

$0 < mpc < 1$ e.g.: the 2016 estimate of the *mpc* of the US is 0.8 (International Monetary Fund)

$a > 0$ e.g.: in 2009, the average household's autonomous consumption was \$17,594 (Krugman and Wells, 2013)

Graphically, on a diagram with Consumption (C) on the vertical axis, and disposable income (Y-T) on the horizontal axis, the *mpc* is the slope of the consumption function, and *a* is the intercept on the vertical axis:

FIGURE 6.5   Consumption function

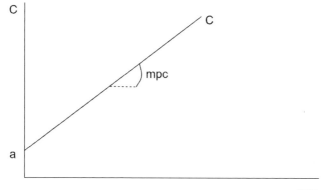

The equation of the consumption function therefore acquires the following expression:

$$C = mpc(Y - T) + a \qquad (6.6)$$

Once we know the consumption function, we can easily derive the (private) saving function. Given that households can only consume or save disposable income:

$$S^{Pr} = (Y - T) - C = (Y - T) - mpc(Y - T) - a = (1 - mpc)(Y - T) - a \ (6.7)$$

Rewriting $(1 - mpc)$ as mps (Marginal Propensity to Save), we obtain:

$$S^{Pr} = mps(Y - T) - a \qquad (6.8)$$

Given that $0 < mpc < 1$, then it must also be that $0 < mps < 1$. And, since $mpc + mps = 1$, then given that $mpc = 0.8$ in 2016 in the US, it then follows that $mps = 0.2$.

Recalling again our fundamental identity between Income and Expenditure approaches, equations (5.1), (5.2), and (5.3):

$Y = AE$ Income (or output) equal to Aggregate Expenditure
$Y = C + G + I$

and substituting the consumption and the investment functions, we obtain:

$$Y = (mpc(Y - T) + a) + G + I(r) \qquad (6.9)$$

In this equation: mpc, a, G, T, the Investment function $I(r)$, and the interest rate r are all given (in the next chapter we will see that the interest rate in the Keynesian model is determined in the nominal – monetary – side of the economy; here we just assume it's already been determined). *The only unknown is Y, the equilibrium level of income (or output).* We then have one equation of degree one with one unknown variable, and the value of our unknown can be found by solving the equation itself.

EXAMPLE

Let:

$mpc = 0.7$
$a = 10$
$G = 100$

$T = 80$

$I = -r + 100$

$r_0 = 10$ (assume that r has already been determined in the nominal side of the economy)

Let's find the equilibrium level of income.

To find the level of investments, plug $r = r_0 = 10$ in the investment function. We obtain:

$I_0 = -r_0 + 100 = -10 + 100 = 90$

Then just plug the values of all our variables in the equilibrium condition:

$Y = mpc(Y - T) + a + I + G$

$Y = 0.7(Y - 80) + 10 + 90 + 100$

$0.3Y = -56 + 200$

$Y^* = \dfrac{144}{0.3} = 480.$

Given: mpc, a, G, T, the investment function $I(r)$, and the interest rate r equal to 10, in this economy, the equilibrium of income (output) Y^* is equal to 480. This means that, given the specifications of our economy, when income is 480, aggregate expenditure is equal to aggregate output (and income).

■ ■ ■

Opportunity for further reflection

Does this equilibrium value of income need to be equal to the full-employment value of income? What is the relationship, if any, between Y^* and $\bar{Y}$?

■ ■ ■

The graphical counterpart of these equations' determination of the equilibrium output is known as the _Keynesian Cross_. You just saw that, once the interest rate is known, aggregate expenditure depends only on income. You also know that equilibrium means Aggregate Expenditure equal to Income.

So, let's set up the Keynesian cross, which you can see in Figure 6.6. We place Y on the horizontal axis, and AE on the vertical axis. Let's also draw a 45^0 ray, along which we would always have $Y = AE$, as the graphical representation of our equilibrium condition. The equilibrium level of income will be found at the intersection between the *AE* line and the 45^0 line. Because public spending (G) and investments (I) do not depend on income, they are represented by straight horizontal lines that intercept the vertical axis at their corresponding values; consumption is a positive function of income, and so is represented by an upward sloping line, with slope equal to the marginal propensity to consume. Notice that the intercept of the consumption function on the vertical axis is at the value $(a - mpcT)$ and not simply (a): this is because we now have (Y) rather than $(Y-T)$ on the horizontal axis (compare it with the consumption function drawn earlier).

FIGURE 6.6   Keynesian model: determination of the equilibrium level of income

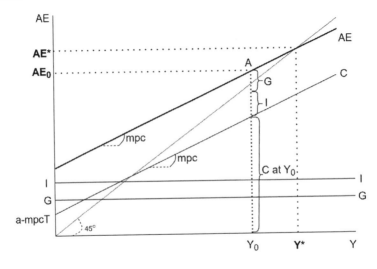

For each possible level of income (say, Y_0), the value of the aggregate expenditure *AE* is equal to the vertical sum of its components *C*, *I*, and *G* at Y_0. The resulting value of aggregate expenditure is the point (A) on the *aggregate expenditure schedule*: at Y_0 the value of the *AE* is AE_0. This calculation can be repeated for any other value of income. Connecting all the points representing the values of AE at different values of income, we obtain a schedule that indicates the *AE* of the economy at any possible level of income. Equilibrium is where aggregate expenditure is equal to income. Notice that the slope of the *AE* is equal to the slope of the consumption function, i.e., *mpc*. The equilibrium level of income (and equilibrium level of AE) is then given by the intersection between the 45^0 ray and the AE schedule: given the specifications of our economy, it is the only level of income (Y^*) that implies a level of aggregate expenditure (AE^*) that is equal to the level of income itself (Y^*).

■ ■ ■

Practice exercise

Draw the Keynesian Cross for the numerical example on the previous page.

■ ■ ■

6.6 Expenditure multipliers

Recall the example introduced earlier:

$mpc = 0.7$
$a = 10$
$G = 100$
$T = 80$
$I = -r + 100$
$r = 10.$

The equilibrium level of income (and of aggregate expenditure) was found to be $Y^* = 480$.

We now ask the question: what is the effect of a change in one (or more) of the autonomous (non-dependent on Y) variables of the economy on the equilibrium level of income? For instance, how does this equilibrium income change if, say, public expenditure G is increased by 100?

At first glance, one would say that aggregate expenditure, and so income, should all increase by 100, because in the aggregate expenditure equation, G has coefficient 1: $Y = AE = C + G + I$. Equilibrium income, however, increases by much more than 100. Let's run the experiment:

First round of expenditures: $\Delta G = 100 \Rightarrow \Delta AE_0 = 100 \Rightarrow \Delta Y_0 = 100$ output adjusts to the increase in AE;

but then:

Second round: $\Delta Y_0 = 100 \Rightarrow \Delta C_0 = .7(\Delta Y_0) = 70 \Rightarrow \Delta AE_1 = 70 \Rightarrow \Delta Y_1 = 70$

Third round: $\Delta Y_1 = 70 \Rightarrow \Delta C_1 = .7(\Delta Y_1) = 49 \Rightarrow \Delta AE_2 = 49 \Rightarrow \Delta Y_2 = 49$

Fourth round: $\Delta Y_2 = 49 \Rightarrow \Delta C_2 = .7(\Delta Y_2) = 34.3 \Rightarrow \Delta AE_3 = 34.3 \Rightarrow \Delta Y_3 = 34.3$

and so on until the process dies out.

Summing up, the total change in aggregate expenditure and income triggered by an initial increase in public expenditure by 100 is:

$$\Delta Y^* = \Delta AE^* = \Delta Y_0 + \Delta Y_1 + \Delta Y_2 + \Delta Y_3 + \ldots$$
$$= \Delta G + 0.7(\Delta G) + 0.7[0.7(\Delta G)] + 0.7[0.7[0.7(\Delta G)]] + \ldots$$
$$= \Delta G[1 + 0.7 + 0.7^2 + 0.7^3 + \ldots]$$

which is known in mathematics as a "geometric sum." Because $mpc = 0.7 < 1$, such a sum can be reduced to:

$$\Delta Y^* = \Delta AE^* = (\frac{1}{1-0.7})\Delta G = 3.33(\Delta G) = 333$$

Thus, in our example, an increase of G by 100 leads to an overall increase in aggregate expenditure and equilibrium income by 333!
   In general, we can write:

$$\Delta Y^* = \Delta AE^* = 1/(1-mpc)\Delta G \qquad\qquad (6.10)$$

The "magnifying factor" $\dfrac{1}{1 - mpc}$ is called the *public expenditure multiplier*.

■ ■ ■

Opportunity for further reflection

What is the intuition behind this "multiplicative effect through consumption" of public expenditure? What does actually happen in real life to aggregate expenditure, income, and consumption, when the government increases public expenditure by a certain amount? Can you imagine this process if the government, for example, decreases taxes instead of increasing public expenditure?

■ ■ ■

In general, any increase in any one or more of the autonomous components of aggregate expenditure (a, G, I, and T) causes a multiplicative effect on aggregate expenditure and income, and thus has a *multiplier* associated with it. In order to find the values of the various multipliers, we can simply rewrite the aggregate expenditure equation bringing all the terms in Y to the left-hand side:

$$Y = mpc(Y - T) + a + I + G$$
$$Y - mpcY = -mpcT + a + I + G$$

$$(1 - mpc)Y = -mpcT + a + I + G$$
$$Y = 1/(1 - mpc)[-mpcT + a + I + G]$$

The expression above can now be used to evaluate the "total" effect on the equilibrium level of income from a variation in the different components of aggregate expenditure, letting them change one at a time.

- An increase or decrease in public expenditures, ΔG, while keeping all the other components of aggregate expenditure fixed (the *ceteris paribus* assumption), leads to the following change in Y (we saw this in the previous page):

  $$\Delta Y = 1/(1 - mpc)[\Delta G] \quad \textit{public expenditure multiplier}$$

- An increase or decrease in taxation, ΔT, while keeping all the other components of aggregate expenditure fixed, leads to the following change in Y (notice the negative sign!):

  $$\Delta Y = -mpc/(1 - mpc)[\Delta T] \quad \textit{taxation multiplier} \tag{6.11}$$

- An increase or decrease in autonomous consumption, Δa, while keeping all the other components of aggregate expenditure fixed, leads to the following change in Y:

  $$\Delta Y = 1/(1 - mpc)[\Delta a] \quad \textit{autonomous consumption multiplier} \tag{6.12}$$

- An increase or decrease in investments, ΔI, while keeping all the other components of aggregate expenditure fixed, leads to the following change in Y:

  $$\Delta Y = 1/(1 - mpc)[\Delta I] \quad \textit{investment multiplier} \tag{6.13}$$

Memorization hint: there is only one expenditure multiplier different from all the others!

PRACTICE EXERCISES

1. Assume:

    $mpc = 0.8$

    $a = 500$

    $T = 1,000$

    $G = 800$

$$I = -0.5r + 1,000$$
$$r = 10$$

Draw the Keynesian Cross and algebraically find the equilibrium level of income. (Solution: $Y^* = 7,475$)

2.   Recall the example given earlier in this section:

$$mpc = 0.7$$
$$a = 10$$
$$G = 100$$
$$T = 80$$
$$I = -r + 100 = 10$$

Suppose that the government wants to increase public expenditure (ΔG) by 200 and wants to pay for it by collecting 200 in additional taxes (ΔT). Will the equilibrium level of income change? If yes, by how much? If no, why? Provide the economic intuition of your result. [Solution: $\Delta Y = 200$, the so-called *balanced budget* multiplier is equal to 1]

6.7 Macroeconomic policy in the Keynesian framework: goods market

What should the main goals of macroeconomic policy be in the Keynesian framework (goods market)? Given that output (or income) can be persistently below or above its full employment level, the most important goal of policy in the Keynesian framework is <u>the stabilization of output as close to the trend as possible, that is, the containment of the depth of recessions and height of booms so as to minimize unemployment in recessions and the possibility of inflation in booms.</u>

Thus, the general policy recipes (<u>in the goods market</u>) in the Keynesian framework are:

1.   When output is below its full-employment level: increase Aggregate Expenditure!
2.   When output is above its full-employment level: decrease Aggregate Expenditure!

1.   Policies that increase Aggregate Expenditure:

   •   *Expansionary* fiscal policy: increase Public Spending (G) and/or decrease Taxation (T);

- Nudge households to consume a higher percentage of their income (encourage an increase in *mpc*) or to increase their autonomous consumption (*a*);
- Nudge firms to invest more, by infusing them with optimism about the future of the economy.

Graphically, each of these policies (or any combination of them) causes a shift upward of the Aggregate Expenditure schedule, and thus a higher level of equilibrium income. Recall:

$$Y = AE = C + G + I$$

In the diagram below, consider, for instance, an increase in public expenditure, ΔG, from G_0 to G_1 (with G_1 higher than G_0), while all the other variables remain constant. The line that represents public expenditure will shift up by ΔG, which will make also the Aggregate Expenditure schedule shift up by the same amount (from AE_0 to AE_1). The intersection between the new Aggregate Expenditure (AE_1) and the 45^0 line will determine an equilibrium level of income $Y_1{}^*$, which is clearly higher than the previous $Y_0{}^*$.

How much higher is $Y_1{}^*$ than $Y_0{}^*$? Apply the public expenditure multiplier:

$$Y_1^* = \frac{1}{1 - mpc} (\Delta G) + Y_0^*.$$

FIGURE 6.7   Keynesian model: effects of an increase in public expenditure

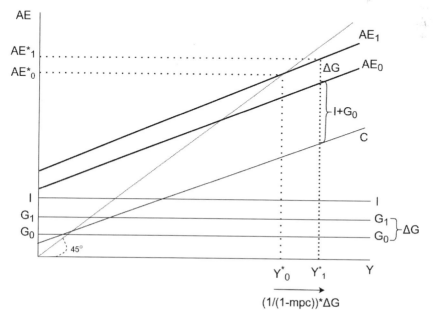

■ ■ ■

Opportunity for further reflection

Finding inspiration from the list of policies aimed at increasing Aggregate Expenditure, create a list of policies (in the goods market) that would "cool down" the economy in a situation of boom.

Practice exercise

Assume the following economy:

$mpc = 0.6$

$a = 500$

$G = 1,500$

$T = 1,500$

$I = -200r + 2,000$ where $r = 5$

Assume also that the full-employment level of income is: $\bar{Y} = 7,500$.

Address the following prompts:

1. Draw the Keynesian Cross that describes this economy.
2. Calculate the short-run level of income Y^*. Is this economy in a recession or a boom?
3. Determine the change in public expenditure (*ceteris paribus*) that would be necessary to bring the level of income to its full-employment level. (Solution: $\Delta G = 900$)
4. Determine the change in Taxation (*ceteris paribus*) that would be necessary to bring the level of income to its full-employment level. (Solution: $\Delta T = -1,500$)

■ ■ ■

Note

1. Data regarding the Great Depression was gathered from Riddel et al., 2011, pp. 319–320 and from the educational webpage of the Federal Reserve Bank of St. Louis (www.stlouisfed.org/education).

References

Andrews, Wilson, Kenan Davis, Adam Pearce, and Nadja Popovich (2017) "What Trump's Tax Proposal Will Cost." *The New York Times*, April 26.

Federal Reserve of St. Louis (2019) "Econ Ed at the St. Louis Fed." www.stlouisfed.org/education.

Krugman, Paul and Robin Wells (2013) *Economics*. New York: Worth Publishers.

Riddel, Tom, Jean Shackelford, Geoffrey Schneider, and Steve Stamos (2011) *Economics. A Tool for Critically Understanding Society*. Ninth Edition, Boston: Addison Wesley.

7

Money changes everything

Macroeconomic theory and policy: the money market

 ## 7.1 What is money?

Working along with the real side of the economy is the monetary system, which enables people to carry out transactions with each other, whether buying or selling, saving or investing, borrowing or lending. At the heart of the monetary system is ... money! While common language gives money several connotations, which range from coins and banknotes to wealth, economists have a precise definition of money: <u>money is perfect liquidity</u>. Operationally, <u>it is the stock of assets that can be legally and readily used to make transactions and hold value</u>. The assets which have acted as money have varied over time, and you'll see different monies in different countries; so, it is important to remember that money changes as the economy changes. In other words, money is what can be used to make and receive payments and store value: in stable times, any commodity generally accepted as means of payment, as a way of settling a debt, can be money; during times of duress, there are fewer acceptable assets.

Usually, money is defined by its three fundamental functions (and, as we'll see later, these functions inform the demand for money).

- <u>Medium of exchange</u>: it is an asset that people are willing to accept as payment for what they sell because they in turn can use it to pay for something else they want. This function is dependent on liquidity.
- <u>Store of value</u>: money is a convenient way to store purchasing power and wealth through time. Money as cash maintains its value over time. This function is, however, affected by inflation.
- <u>Unit of account</u>: money provides a convenient means to express the value of goods and services (prices).

Following the definition of money as *anything* that is generally accepted to settle a debt, the most used definition of money is the sum of <u>currency</u> (cash) and <u>checking deposits</u>; and <u>the sum of currency and checking deposits held</u>

by the public is the most common definition of *money supply* (M^S). This definition of money, however, is sometimes too narrow: for instance, think about the purchase of some real estate or a company, for which one can also pay with certificate of deposits (time deposits), treasury bonds, ownership shares (stocks), and perhaps other forms of savings. In order to also take these different possibilities into account, it is customary to distinguish among different definitions of money supply. Each of these depends on the degree of liquidity, where *degree of liquidity* stands for *acceptability as means of payment* or *ease of conversion to cash.*

To introduce the different aspects and definitions of the money supply, we start with the Monetary Base and then introduce the two additional categories. Beginning with the narrowest definition and proceeding according to decreasing liquidity, we have:

MB   Currency held in the vaults of financial institutions and reserves held by the Central Bank (the Federal Reserve, or Fed, in the US).

M1   Currency held by the public + checkable deposits + travelers' checks.

M2   M1 + deposits for which the possibility of writing checks is more limited, such as saving accounts, time deposits (short maturity), and money market mutual fund shares.

As said earlier, the most common definition of Money Supply is: M1, even though the Fed uses M2.

The Federal Reserve (Federal Reserve, Tables H-3 and H-6) collects data on these categories and what follows should give you an idea of their respective magnitudes in the US.

MB: $3,244.5 billion in May 2019;

M1: $3,784.0 billion in May 2019; and

M2: $14,632.8 billion in May 2019.

▉ 7.2 Money creation

While you may have thought that money was created simply by being printed, there are actually several different and important institutions in the process of creating money.

Central Banks – the Federal Reserve System (Fed) in the US, the Bank of England in the United Kingdom, the European Central Bank in the Euro Zone, and so on – are the only institutions authorized to issue their respective currency. So, the American currency, the US dollar, can be legally issued only by the Fed, as the euro can only be issued by the European Central

Bank. But because currency is not the only component of money supply, commercial banks, such as Citibank or Bank of America, also play an essential role in the determination of the money supply of a country. When people deposit funds into their checking and saving accounts, banks can lend these funds to individuals and firms who want to borrow them. This process of lending leads to an expansion of checking deposit funds.

The key aspects of the structure of the Federal Reserve System can be summarized as follows:

Board of Governors	District Federal Reserve Banks
* It is located in Washington DC; * Seven governors nominated to 14-year terms by the President of the US, and confirmed by the Senate; * One governor is nominated as chair by the President of the US, for a 4-year term. Jerome Powell is the current chair of the Board of Governors. * A staff of professional economists and statisticians provide the data and information needed for the Fed to make monetary policy.	* 12 Federal Reserve Banks are located in different regions of the country (Boston, NYC, Philadelphia, Richmond, Atlanta, Cleveland, Chicago, St. Louis, Kansas City, Minneapolis, Dallas, San Francisco); * Each district bank is headed by a president chosen by commercial bankers of the district, and approved by the Board of Governors; * The Federal Reserve Bank of New York has special responsibilities in carrying out decisions made by the Fed.

Federal Open Market Committee (FOMC)

* Meets every six weeks in DC, and makes decisions about monetary policy and modalities of implementation
* Consists of the Board of Governors and five district bank presidents (on a rotating basis)
* Each person has one vote, but it is known that the Chair of the Board of Governors has considerably more power than that one vote might represent

While the Fed is most commonly associated with US monetary policy, it is also a key regulator of the commercial banks. Its rules address the safety and soundness of the financial system.

Commercial banks are private firms, which, like all other firms, pursue the objective of profit maximization. Banks maximize profits in two fundamental ways:

• they maximize the difference between the interest rate they receive from loans and the interest rate they pay on deposits as well as by charging fees for their services;

- they maximize the amount of loans they give out, given the amount of deposits they acquire.

There is an interesting relationship between deposits and loans. Commercial banks do not need to keep all of the acquired deposits ready for withdrawal. Clients typically keep their deposits for relatively long periods of time, and banks certainly don't want to miss profit opportunities by keeping idle money in their vaults. Banks need to keep just a portion of their deposits ready for withdrawal, in what is known as reserves: the rest can be safely lent out. The important decision that has to be made is, of course, the determination of the portion of deposits that has to be kept as reserve, that is, the determination of the reserve ratio: the lower the ratio is, the higher the capacity of commercial banks to create money (through loans), but the more likely it is that when people decide to withdraw their deposits, they don't "find money" at the bank. The reserve ratio is simply given by the amount of reserves divided by the amount of deposits:

$$Reserve\,Ratio = \frac{Reserves}{Deposits}$$

It is the Fed that puts a floor on the whole mechanism: a lower limit on the size of the reserve ratio, which is called the _required_ reserve ratio. It is this decision on the size of the required reserve ratio that allows the Fed to exert control over the activity of commercial banks and the levels of M1 and M2.

This reserve ratio relationship also helps us see how the Fed can affect the money supply.

r = Required reserve ratio
R = Required reserves
D = Deposits

$$r = R/D \qquad\qquad\qquad\qquad\qquad (7.1)$$

$$D = \left(\frac{1}{r}\right)R \qquad\qquad\qquad\qquad\qquad (7.2)$$

As equation 7.2 shows, the Fed affects the money creation process of commercial banks in different ways.

- The Fed can change the required reserve ratio. In equation 7.2, $1/r$ is known as the money multiplier. A change in R is multiplied by $1/r$ to either increase or decrease D;.
- Commercial banks can "borrow reserves" from the Fed, to enable themselves to lend out more of their deposits. The Fed can encourage/discourage borrowing by commercial banks by changing the interest

rate it charges them. The interest rate charged by the Fed to commercial banks is called the *discount rate*: the higher the discount rate is, the higher the cost of borrowing for commercial banks is, the higher the interest rate they need to charge to their customers is, and so the lower the total amount that commercial banks are able to lend.

As mentioned earlier, the Fed affects the money supply of the US not only by setting reserve ratios (and so loans) of commercial banks, but also by regulating the amount of currency held by the public. Recall that the currency which is part of the money supply (M1, M2) is only the currency in circulation, that is, currency not held in the vaults of the Fed. Any operation of the Fed that either withdraws currency from the public or increases currency held by the public is also a change in money supply.

The main way in which the Fed changes the amount of currency held by the public is known as Open Market Operations (OMO). OMO mainly consist of the purchase or sale of treasury bonds by the Fed through bond market specialists. By purchasing bonds, the Fed increases the money supply by paying the private individuals (or the government) who are selling bonds to the Fed; by selling bonds the Fed is paid with currency previously held by the public (in other words, OMO make currency either leave or return to the vaults of the Fed). These bond sales/purchases can also affect deposits if the funds are deposited or withdrawn from bank accounts.

In conclusion, the Fed can affect the money supply through its instruments and regulations, and when the Fed modifies this supply or Fed controlled interest rates, we say that the Fed engages in monetary policy. Its policies have fundamental implications for the whole economy, both in the long-run and in the short-run. We will first analyze the impact of the money supply in the long-run on the economy, with the Quantity Equation of Money of the Classical model, and then proceed with the analysis in the short-run by studying the Keynesian money market, that will show the effects of changes in the money supply on the short-run macroeconomic equilibrium.

■ ■ ■

Opportunity for further reflection

1. What makes money different from other financial assets?
2. Clarify within yourself the difference between *fiscal policy* and *monetary policy*: be clear about what the variables in question are in the two *types* of policy, and about the institutions that are responsible for policy decisions and implementation.

3. Why do all economies have non-market institutions to "control" and manage the money supply?
4. Explain the ways in which the Fed could increase the money supply.

■ ■ ■

 ## 7.3 Classical theory: the quantity identity (and theory) of money

The fundamental assumption of this approach to money is that the only function of money is to facilitate transactions (this will make more sense once you see the difference between this approach and the Keynesian one). Because people use money to buy and sell goods and services, and because, in the economy-as-a-whole, nominal GDP is the current dollar value of all goods and services, we expect to see a close relationship between money supply and nominal income (nominal GDP). This relationship is expressed by:

$$M \times V = P \times Y \qquad \textit{Quantity Identity of Money} \qquad (7.3)$$

where:

M: average money supply in a given year;
V: velocity of money, during the same period of time;
P: price level, during the same period of time; and
Y: real GDP (real output, or real income) of the given year.

The *quantity identity* is always true because of the definition of velocity: the rate at which money moves through the economy during a given period, or the number of times a piece of money gets spent:

$$V = \frac{P \times Y}{M} \qquad (7.4)$$

Since national income is a measure of all output (Y) in a country for a year multiplied by the price (P) of each good or service, V is equal, in effect, to national income in a given year divided by the total amount of money available (on average) during that year. In 2019, for instance, V was equal to 1.44, with a money supply (M2) of $14,632.8 billion and a first quarter 2019 nominal GDP of $21,098.8 billion:

$$V = 1.44 = \frac{21,098.8B}{14,632.8B} \qquad$$ (Federal Reserve; U.S. Bureau of Economic Analysis).

The idea of the Quantity Identity of Money, introduced by the British philosopher John Locke in the seventeenth century, was further elaborated by the Scottish philosopher David Hume during the following century, and became the main conceptualization of money during the Classical period of political economy. Milton Friedman, leading economist of the Chicago School of economics and of the Monetarist School, in the late 1950s turned the Quantity *Identity* into a Quantity *Theory* by adding the assumption that, when money is defined as M2, the Velocity of Money can be taken as constant. Velocity depends on institutional factors, so it was hypothesized to change only when they do. In addition, Friedman utilized the Classical, long-run paradigm that assumes that output is always at full-employment, and strictly determined by the resources and technology of the economy.

Thus, Friedman (and monetarists after him) operated according to the following three assumptions:

- Money Supply is defined as M2;
- Velocity of Money is constant (for M2); and
- Real GDP, Y, is always at full-employment: $Y = \bar{Y}$ (which makes this a Classical, long-run theory).

If you now look at the quantity identity more carefully, you notice that *if velocity is constant*, then an increase in the money supply will be fully reflected in an increase in the nominal GDP, i.e., $P \times Y$. Nominal GDP can increase because the price level changes and/or because the real GDP changes. But because $Y = \bar{Y}$, and $\bar{Y}$ does not depend on the Money Supply ($\bar{Y}$ depends on those variables that expand the Production Possibility Frontier, as discussed in Chapter 2), the strict relationship between money supply and nominal GDP reduces in fact to a <u>direct relationship between money supply and general level of prices</u>. To see it, we need to move from the Quantity Identity in levels given above to the rates of growth of its components. The mathematical rule that transforms products into sums of rates of growth is as follows:

given $ab = cd$ where a, b, c, d are four variables, we obtain:

$$\hat{a} + \hat{b} = \hat{c} + \hat{d}$$

where the "hat" on each variable indicates its rate of growth (its percentage change through time).

Applying this rule to $M \times V = P \times Y$, we get:

$$\hat{M} + \hat{V} = \hat{P} + \hat{Y} \tag{7.5}$$

where:

$\hat{M}$:   rate of growth of money supply;

$\hat{V}$:   rate of change of velocity. If velocity is constant, its rate of growth is zero ($\hat{V} = 0$);

$\hat{P}$:   rate of growth of prices, that is, the inflation rate; and

$\hat{Y}$:   rate of growth of full-employment output (given exogenously by the rate of growth of resources and technology).

This equation states that if money supply grows, say, at 7% a year, velocity is constant, and the growth rate of full-employment output is, say, 3%, then there will be an inflation rate of 4%! To obtain a lower rate of inflation, the rate of growth of money supply needs to be reduced: if money supply grows at 4%, for instance, the inflation rate will be only 1%.

Because the money supply and its growth rate are largely determined by the Fed, the Quantity Theory is therefore a powerful tool for monetary authorities to determine the inflation rate (on the trend). This is also known as the *monetarist rule*, which says that *because in the long-run inflation is a purely monetary phenomenon, then the task of the central bank is (only) to determine the rate of growth of money supply that leads to the desired inflation rate*. Don't forget that this rule is completely based on the three assumptions mentioned earlier as the foundation of the Quantity Theory.

One additional consequence of this approach to money is that changes in the money supply do not affect the real level of output (and income). In the Classical theory, the *real* and the *nominal* sides of the economy are held completely separate: this is known as the *Classical dichotomy*.

■ ■ ■

Practice exercise

The Fed's current monetary policy has an inflation rate target of 2% and the real economy is growing at around 2%. What is the money supply growth rate that would produce the desired policy result? Do you think that credit has an impact on expenditures in the economy? Credit expenditures rose by 5.2% in May 2019, how could they affect the Fed's policies with respect to the money supply?

■ ■ ■

7.4 The Central Bank and the interest rate: the Keynesian monetary system

When we abandon the Classical, long-run idea that output is always at full-employment (that the economy is on the trend), the story changes quite a bit.

Every time the Federal Open Market Committee (FOMC) meets, newspapers report on the decision of the FOMC to increase, decrease, or maintain the prevailing interest rate. Yet, you have not learned that the Fed "changes the interest rate" (with the exception of the discount rate): you learned that the Fed affects the money supply (that is, the money in circulation and the extent to which commercial banks can lend). What you learned is, in fact, correct: the Fed can only act on the money supply or parts of it, but by doing so it drives the interest rate up or down. In the short-run, the interest rate is determined in the money market, which consists – as any other market – of a demand and a supply: the money demand and the money supply. The demand for money is closely tied to the functions that money plays.

[For the sake of good memorization and clarity: where and how is the interest rate determined in the Classical model?]

Money demand (M^D) can be defined as the amount of money people keep in their pocket and in their checking accounts, which is the purchasing power people want to keep ready for use as well as for psychological security, multiplied by the price level.

Each of us has to make this decision pretty often, and the factors we take into account in the determination of our money demand typically are:

- How much, in terms of goods and services and their prices, we want to buy. The amount of goods and services we want to buy depends on how much income we have, as the higher income is, the higher consumption is. There is, therefore, a positive relationship between the level of income and the amount of liquidity (purchasing power) we want to hold. We call this component of the money demand *transactions demand*, and it is tied to its function as a means of payment and a unit of account. This was the only function of money in the Classical model.

- How much we want to hold to meet unforeseen expenses, for a *rainy day*. Liquidity can reduce the impact of uncertainty, so there is a reason to hold money for its own sake. How much we hold for this purpose is also a positive function of the level of income: the higher our level of income is, the more purchasing power we want to hold ready for anything unforeseen. We call this component of the money demand *precautionary demand*, and it is also tied to its function as a store of value.

- How much we lose by holding money rather than keeping our wealth in interest-bearing assets, such as saving accounts or bonds. This is the act of holding money because it is the perfectly liquid asset even though it is non-interest bearing. The <u>interest rate</u> can be thought of as the *opportunity cost* of holding money: it is what we give up by holding money in our pocket or checking account instead of keeping it in an interest-bearing asset. A higher interest rate makes it more costly for us to hold money in our pocket, because we lose more. There is a <u>negative relation between the level of the interest rate and the amount of liquidity we want to hold</u>. We call this component of money demand *speculative demand,* and it is also tied to money's function as a store of value.

<u>Thus, money demand is a positive function of prices and income, and a negative function of the interest rate</u>.
   Algebraically, money demand can be expressed in the following form:

$$M^D = P \times f(r, Y). \tag{7.6}$$

Given the level of prices, the money demand schedule, $M^D = f(r, Y; P)$, seen in Figure 7.1, represents the negative relationship between the amount of money individuals want to hold and the interest rate, at each particular

FIGURE 7.1   Money demand

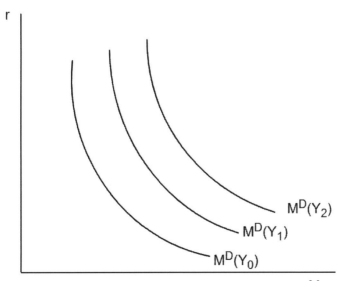

level of income and price level. The higher the level of income is, the higher the amount of transactions people want to pay for is, and so the higher the money demand is (at constant prices). Graphically, assuming $Y_2 > Y_1 > Y_0$, then Figure 7.1 shows the increase in M^D as Y increases.

Equilibrium in the money market means, as always, quantity supplied equal to quantity demanded, which happens at the intersection of demand and supply. The money supply can be easily super-imposed in the graph above: remember that the money supply is a policy decision by the Fed. Because money supply does not depend on the level of the interest rate, it appears in the graph, Figure 7.2, as a vertical line, that corresponds to the amount of money the Fed wants in circulation. Assume for a moment that income is given at a level Y_0.

FIGURE 7.2   Money market equilibrium

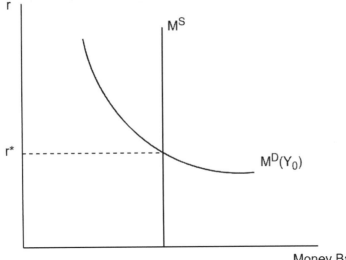

Then, as you can see, there is only one level of the interest rate that keeps the money market in equilibrium, *given* a certain level of prices, income, and money supply: r^*. This specific interest rate is called the short-run *equilibrium interest rate*.

EXAMPLE

Let:

$M^S = 800$

$M^D = 5(-100r + 0.5Y)$, where 5 represents the general level of prices.

Suppose that the equilibrium level of real income is $Y = 1,000$, then, the Money Market Equilibrium, obtained by equating M^S to M^D, is given by:

$800 = 5(-100r + 500)$

$800 = -500r + 2,500$

$500r = 1700$

$r^* = 3.4$, the equilibrium interest rate.

It should now be easy to see how the Fed can "control" the interest rate by acting on the money supply.

■ ■ ■

Practice exercise

Suppose that the Fed performs an open market operation and buys bonds in the bond market. Keeping the price level and income fixed (for the moment), explain verbally and graphically the effect of such operation in the money market, and the consequence of it on the equilibrium interest rate.

■ ■ ■

But let's now see how this monetary view of interest rates affects the real economy.

Given that:

- monetary policy (changes in the Money Supply implemented by the Fed) affects the interest rate,
- the interest rate affects the level of investments,
- investments are a component of Aggregate Expenditure, and
- Aggregate Expenditure in the Keynesian model determines the level of output (and income)...

it follows that, <u>in the Keynesian view, and in general in the short-run, there is *no dichotomy* between the real and nominal side of the economy, and *monetary policy can be effective on the level of output and thus on the rate of unemployment*</u>.

As you can see in Figure 7.3, there is now a link between the Money Market graph and the Keynesian Cross, via the Investments schedule! Let's suppose that the Fed buys bonds in an Open Market Operation.

Figure 7.3 shows graphically how this expansionary monetary policy produces an increase in the money supply. As we have noted, the monetary

FIGURE 7.3 Money market equilibrium and determination of investment
expenditures

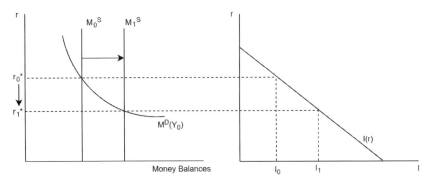

and real sides of the economy come together in the Keynesian view. Now, we
can use the information from the previous example to show mathematically
how the increase in the level of the money supply produced a lower interest rate, which when found on the investment function is associated with a
higher level of investment.

EXAMPLE

Let:

$$M_1^S = 1,000$$
$$M^D = 5(-100r + 0.5Y)$$

As in the previous example, we will keep the level of Y constant, so Y = 1,000.
By substituting in the known values we get the following:

$$1,000 = -500r + 2500$$
$$500r = 2500 - 1000$$
$$r_1{}^* = \frac{1500}{500}$$
$$r_1{}^* = 3.0$$

We can now see that if the Fed were to buy bonds, which would increase the
money supply, the level of the interest rate would fall and the level of investment would rise. Money does change everything!

■ ■ ■

Practice exercises

1.   Draw a generic money market and a generic Keynesian Cross (draw all the components of AE, and the AE schedule). Notice that the interest rate determined in the money market is the determinant of the level of Investments you have on the Keynesian Cross. Assume that the economy is in a recession. Show in three separate sets of money market and Keynesian Cross graphs the effects of the following policy interventions:

- the government intervenes with an appropriate change in Public Spending (ΔG), *ceteris paribus*
- the government intervenes with an appropriate change in Taxation (ΔT), *ceteris paribus*
- the Fed intervenes with an appropriate change in the Money Supply (ΔM^S), *ceteris paribus*

2.   Do the same exercise with the assumption that the economy is in a boom.

■ ■ ■

▨ References

Federal Reserve Board of Governors. "Aggregate Reserves of Depository Institutions and Monetary Base-H-3." Accessed on 8/7/2019: https://www.federalreserve.gov/releases/h3/current/default.htm.

Federal Reserve Board of Governors. "Money Stock and Debt Measures-H-6." Accessed on 8/7/2019: https://www.federalreserve.gov/releases/h6/current/default.htm.

US Bureau of Economic Analysis. "Table 1.1.6 Gross Domestic Product." Accessed on 7/4/2019 https://apps.bea.gov/iTable/iTable.cfm?reqid=19&step=2#reqid=19&step=2&isuri=1&1921=survey.

8 The embedded economy

▨ 8.1 Introduction

Hopefully, you remember that the first chapter of this book described the Classical political economy's focus on the creation of wealth, also known as value, as having captured the minds of these early economists. It also described how important differences among economists arose from their varied ideological, methodological (view of scientific process), and paradigmatic approaches. In the chapters that followed, the tenets of the Neoclassical paradigm were explained, and now, we will introduce you to an alternative economic view that once again emphasizes the creation of value. This model, however, embeds the economy in a social and physical context, which means that it adopts a different paradigm and ideological approach from the Neoclassical model. Using this alternative context, we will in the rest of this chapter present some of the social challenges that we face today. The alternative model draws on the notion of an *embedded economy*.

This idea accepts that the monetized economy, or the parts of the economy captured in statistics like GDP, relies on activities that take place in other areas of society (Jochimsen and Knoblock, 1997; Dengler and Strunk, 2018). Figure 8.1 shows how this works. Notice that, in some ways, this is quite similar to some of the flow diagrams described in Chapter 5, but we have rearranged and added a few things to highlight some relationships that were previously obscured or left out. Households are the key economic actor in society, where they are responsible for reproducing labor. In order to do this, they purchase what they need from the monetized economy to consume or produce things in the household. Social norms and institutions (like laws and customs) shape who is expected to do what. Note that the monetized economy is *embedded* in society, meaning that it does not exist outside of it. Norms and institutions shape what happens in markets and through government spending; indeed, markets and regulations are institutions themselves and are socially constructed.

FIGURE 8.1   The embedded economy

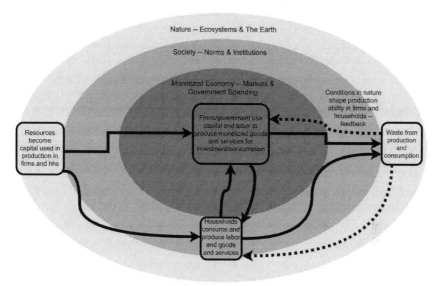

Both the monetized economy and society are physically located within nature. The planet and all of its physical systems provide resources that can be turned into capital, services like clean air that allow for production to take place (and hinder it when not present), and amenities that are valuable for their own sake, like being able to go hiking in a National Park for fun. Households in traditional societies and developing countries that are heavily dependent on agriculture are more directly reliant on taking resources from the environment for household production. As ecological economists note, *all* matter and energy that is taken from nature and moved through the economic/social system eventually returns to the environment as waste. If too much waste accumulates in nature, the economic system's ability to produce might be hindered, as in the case of anthropogenic (human-caused) climate change. We will discuss some of the implications of viewing the economy this way, starting with some important contributions from feminist economics.

8.2 Feminist economics

As you've seen in Chapters 5 and 6, the primary measure of the income (value) generated within an economy is the Gross Domestic Product (GDP), but it only counts market-mediated economic activities, which means the laboring of many groups is omitted.[1] Think about the work that is done in the home for no wage: cooking meals, dishwashing, house cleaning, house, lawn, and garden maintenance, clothes cleaning and maintenance, child care, as well as elder care. Think also about the many thousands of hours of volunteer workers whose labor is also valued at zero. Yet, when these same activities are engaged in for wages, they are counted in GDP. So, it is not the lack of value of the activities that renders them valueless; it is their social context that obviates their value. This omission in our measurement of economic activity has a disproportionate effect on the contribution that women make to economic activity and development. As you may recall from looking at the American Time Use Survey in Chapter 5, it is women who provide by far the largest amount of labor in this sphere of unpaid home production, so it is their economic role that is being obscured. This lopsided understanding of how and where value is created is one of the key inequalities on which feminist economists focus.

Creation of value

Feminist economists today argue that activities of production within the household have value, and in an earlier economic history period they were also considered productive and included as an important portion of production. Today's traditional measures of economic activity count this unpaid work as "unproductive" activity. By categorizing house work (primarily women's work) as "unproductive," it set up an argument for women's work, in general, as not being work and, therefore, in an economy focused on generating value (income and wealth), threw the cloak of invisibility over women's actual contributions to an economy's well-being (Waring, 1988).

In the diagram of our alternative economy, Figure 8.1, we see how the household is embedded in the economy as well as the society. Along with being consumers, which is emphasized in Chapter 6, households must also be considered for their value-creating activities if we are to get a complete view of the operation of our economic system. We, therefore, need to include in our understanding of economic activity the totality of productive engagement – all work that creates value. Time use surveys have been introduced to specifically acknowledge and provide data on households' unpaid economic activity and understand who is actively engaged in its creation.

Let's see how much of an impact unpaid home work has on an economy. Utilizing time use surveys, the United Nations (2015) gathered data on work hours of people in developed and developing economies. See Table 8.1. From these data you can see that both men and women spend time doing unpaid work in the home (along with their paid work). They are both engaged in creating value that is visible as well as invisible, but is that creation generated equally?

TABLE 8.1   Hours (minutes) spent daily on paid and unpaid work by sex, developing and developed countries, 2005–2013

Developing countries	Market work – paid	Home work – unpaid	Total
Women	2:35 (155)	4:34 (274)	7:09 (429)
Men	4:58 (298)	1:18 (78)	6:16 (376)
Total	7:33 (453)	5:52 (352)	13:25 (805)
Developed countries			
Women	2:25 (145)	4:20 (260)	6:45 (405)
Men	3:56 (236)	2:16 (136)	6:12 (372)
Total	6:21 (381)	6:36 (396)	12:57 (777)

Source: United Nations, 2015. *The World's Women 2015: Trends and Statistics.* New York: United Nations, Department of Economic and Social Affairs, Statistics Division.

Looking at the data, we see that in developing countries men and women create on average 352 minutes (5 hours 52 minutes) of unseen value per day. Looking at this expenditure of time in the context of men and women's total work time, 805 minutes (13 hours 25 minutes), we see that on average unpaid home work accounts for 44 percent of the total value created daily in developing countries. It is perhaps surprising to see that in developed countries the percentage is even higher. On average the total minutes of work for men and women is 777 (12 hours 57 minutes) while the total amount of unpaid work time is 396 minutes (6 hours 36 minutes). This means that 51 percent of all work is unseen. These data indicate that both men and women's unpaid labor has a major effect on an economy.

Taking our analysis one step further, we can see that in both types of countries there is not an even distribution of paid and unpaid work. It is women's work that accounts for most of the unpaid value that is created. In developing countries, women's work is 78 percent (274/352) of the total unpaid home work and in developed countries, it is 66 percent (260/396). Seeing the size of women's unpaid work may help you see how important women are as economic actors, and the reason their contributions are often neglected has to do with the site of their activities, not their value. Including just women's unpaid work in the measurement of economic activities in developing countries would boost it by at least 34 percent (274/805) and by 33 percent (260/777) in developed countries. That's significant.

By acknowledging this invisible work, the usual story about men working more than women can no longer be supported. We see that women are engaged in more total hours of work each day on average than men. By acknowledging the value created in the household, the important contributions made by women's work become visible.

Discrimination – race, ethnicity, and gender

Feminist economists also focus a lot of their research on the problem of discrimination, especially as it is manifested in the labor market. This is the discrimination that is often recounted annually in March or April on Equal Pay Day (in 2019: April 2, for all women), the day that symbolizes how many more days women have to work to make a wage equal to what men earned in the previous year. When these data are disaggregated by race and ethnicity, the dates change: March 5 for Asian women; April 19 for white women; August 22 for Black women; September 23 for Native women; and November 20 for Latinx women (National Committee on Pay Equity). Clearly, race intersects with gender to affect how different groups of women have different labor market experiences. This wage discrimination is measured by the gender pay gap, which shows the difference between the pay men and women who have full-time year-round jobs receive. In 1980 this gap was 40 percent. Now, almost 40 years later the gap has been halved. In recent years, it ranges between 18 and 20 percent – but it persists. And it persists, again, differently for different groups of women (Hegewisch and Hartmann, 2019).

Feminist economists are interested in the full range of questions that involve our economy. We have presented just a couple of the most high-profile problems they tackle.

■ ■ ■

Opportunity for further reflection

Recently, the US Women's Soccer team won their third World Cup, while the US Men's Soccer team has never won a World Cup or made it to the finals. Even with this stunning set of accomplishments, the members of the women's team are paid far less than the members of the men's team. In fact, they are for the second time pursuing a legal case to secure pay equity. What role might you see social and cultural norms playing in *sustaining* this wage gap?

■ ■ ■

▌ 8.3 Ecological economics

In Chapter 3, we discussed the idea of market failures, including the idea that pollution can be considered an externality in a market transaction that should be taxed in order to be "corrected." This is the approach favored by most environmental economists using the Neoclassical model we developed in previous chapters. However, ecological economists argue that, while such taxes may be an important *part* of solving environmental problems, they will inevitably be insufficient. Instead, they argue that firm boundaries must be placed on the scale of the economic system so that it does not overwhelm the functioning of the environmental system and, ultimately, undermine itself.

One example of this thinking is the Planetary Boundaries approach, led by Johann Rockström and others at the Stockholm Resilience Centre. It seeks to lay out "a safe operating space for humanity based on the intrinsic biophysical processes that regulate the stability of the Earth system" (Steffen et al., 2015, p. 736). The approach lists nine planetary boundaries, including things such as having clean freshwater, maintaining the ozone layer, and making sure humans do not overwhelm the land use of natural ecosystems. Two of the nine boundaries are considered "core," climate change and biosphere integrity (that is, biodiversity), which could, if breached on their own, "drive the Earth system into a new state" (Steffen et al., 2015, p. 736). This suggests, for example, that carbon dioxide concentration in the atmosphere should not exceed 350 parts per million (Garver and Goldberg, 2015).[2] Because resource use and waste production cannot grow infinitely without leading to ecological disaster by crossing these boundaries, implementing policies to make the economic system more sustainable becomes crucial.

Recognizing growing threats to the environmental system, the United Nations' World Commission on Environment and Development was asked to discuss strategies for global sustainable development in what became a ground-breaking report in 1987. The report, formally called *Our Common Future*, is more typically referred to as the Brundtland Report after Gro Harlem Brundtland, a former Norwegian prime minister who served as chair of the Commission. The report defined sustainable development as that which "meets the needs of the present without compromising the ability of future generations to meet their own needs" (Brundtland, 1987, I.4).

In practice, however, huge differences have emerged among policymakers, activists, and economists over what this means. Economists using the Neoclassical approach have argued that it is only the total level of capital (human-made and natural) that needs to be preserved, rather than any one particular thing (Solow, 1993). Therefore, if resources can be exploited, turned into human-made capital, and used to achieve the same or better standard of living, it's acceptable.

Ecological economists, on the other hand, point out that there are surely limits to this. Ecological economist Herman Daly uses the example of fish and fishing boats to illustrate the point:

> Man-made capital cannot substitute for natural capital. Once, catches were limited by the number of fishing boats (man-made capital) at sea ... Today the limit is the number of fish in the ocean ... building more boats will

not increase catches. To ensure long-term economic health, nations must sustain the levels of natural capital (such as fish), not just total wealth. (2005, p. 102)

There may thus be cases in which natural and humanmade capital are not good substitutes for one another, and natural capital must be specially preserved. More generally, ecological economists argue that the limits on resource use and waste accumulation in the environmental system should be more clearly understood so that societies can avoid causing irreparable harm to the environment and damage to communities.

Because the environmental system is extremely complex, ecological economists also typically accept that there is a degree of uncertainty regarding our limits. We do not know *exactly* how much environmental harm can be inflicted before we reach a point of no return, and so we should be cautious and humble in setting limits on the economic system. Ecologists have long referred to this idea as the precautionary principle, and ecological economists have advocated for its adoption into economics, too. For example, economist Frank Ackerman argued that climate change, rather than being thought of as an externality problem to be solved, should be thought of in terms of *risk*. That is, with global warming projected to reach certain levels (likely between 3 and 4°C above preindustrial averages by 2100 unless significant action is taken), we can estimate a range of economic damages that this would cause. However, there is some risk that the damage will be truly catastrophic, perhaps by setting off an uncontrollable cycle of warming that would ultimately warm the planet by 6 to 10°C relatively quickly. While this may be unlikely, it would make sense, given the high stakes, for humanity to pay to *be sure* that they avoid that outcome. Ackerman points out that we make decisions like this all the time.

> The annual number of residential fires in the U.S. is about 0.4 percent of the number of housing units. This means that a fire occurs, on average, about once every 250 years in each home, not even close to once per lifetime. By far the most likely number of fires you will experience next year, or even in your lifetime, is zero. Why don't these statistics inspire you to cancel your fire insurance? Unless you are extremely wealthy, the loss of your home in a fire would be a devastating financial blow; despite the low probability, you cannot afford to take any chances on it. (2009, p. 31)

What sorts of solutions do ecological economists advocate for, beyond setting limits on the scale of the economy? There is substantial variation here, with some arguing that, once limits are in place, the market system should be left to work efficiently. Others, however, say that this does not go far enough to ultimately protect the environment. Citing the finite nature of resources and the dangers of overproducing waste, they call for the "degrowth" of the economy, that is, changing the way the economy is organized in order to use fewer resources while still producing high levels of well-being. As one text on degrowth puts it, "in a degrowth society, everything will be different: different activities, different forms and uses of energy, different relations, different gender roles, different allocations of time between paid and non-paid work, different relations with the non-human world" (Kallis, Demaria, and D'Alisa, 2015, p. 4).

More concretely, world leaders adopted the United Nations' Sustainable Development Goals at a summit in 2015 that set out 17 goals designed to promote sustainable development (as defined by the Brundtland Report discussed above) by 2030. These goals intimately link issues such as mitigating climate change and maintaining the health of the world's oceans to eliminating poverty, improving gender equality, and making available affordable and clean energy. Each goal has a number of agreed-upon targets and indicators to measure progress (United Nations, 2019).

■ ■ ■

Opportunity for further reflection

- Do you believe that the *externality view* of climate change or the *insurance view* of climate change is more useful in solving the problem? Why?
- What are some examples of economic activities that you think would become more common in a world that adopts degrowth policies? What kinds of things would become less common? Do you believe such a society is feasible or desirable to work towards?

■ ■ ■

8.4 Putting it together: the beginning of economic wisdom

You may be wondering how the different approaches that you have learned in reading this book can coexist. You may be saying to yourself, "I thought this book would tell me what economics is, not explain things to me and then say they're wrong!" But that's the wrong way to think about this, for a couple of reasons. First, economics is an exciting, evolving, and rich discipline with a variety of perspectives. Economists have many disagreements (even among Neoclassicals), but that makes things interesting! As you have seen, in recent decades, perspectives in economics have been broadened by including concerns about discrimination and the environment further into the discipline (though it still has a long way to go).

Additionally, these frameworks are not necessarily mutually exclusive. Many feminist economists consider themselves Neoclassical economists, too, and they study issues such as the gender wage gap using extensions of the theories discussed in Chapters 3 and 4. Ecological economists may argue that boundaries need to be set on the extent of the economic system, but within that system, many adhere to the Neoclassical paradigm. And, increasingly, ecological and feminist economists are collaborating to discuss ideas about value and well-being (how can we best use limited resources to help the most people?), to understand how to build a socially and environmentally sustainable society and to better understand the disparate impact that environmental disasters have on men and women. Macroeconomics has its own subdisciplines and crossovers that we have not had a chance to discuss in this text, too.

We hope that this brief introduction to economics has inspired you to continue investigating the ideas presented here and asking questions about them. Economics is a field that draws on many skills, which means that all sorts of people can find an interesting place in it. As John Maynard Keynes (1924 [1933]) noted in his obituary for his teacher, Alfred Marshall (the inventor of the supply and demand framework), in the unfortunately gender non-inclusive language of the day:

> The master-economist must possess a rare combination of gifts .... He must be mathematician, historian, statesman, philosopher—in some degree. He must understand symbols and speak in words. He must contemplate the particular, in terms of the general, and touch abstract and concrete in the same flight of thought. He must study the present in the light of the past for the purposes of the future. No part of man's nature or his institutions must be entirely outside his regard. He must be purposeful and disinterested in a simultaneous mood, as aloof and incorruptible as an artist, yet sometimes as near to earth as a politician. (p. 170)

Notes

1. The exceptions to this market-mediated valuation process in GDP are how owner-occupied residences and most of government activity is valued. Since these activities are not usually market-based, their values are imputed using different statistical techniques (Goodwin, Nelson, Harris, 2009, pp. 135–136).
2. Global carbon dioxide concentration reached 414.7 parts per million in May 2019 (NOAA, 2019).

References

Ackerman, Frank (2009) *Can We Afford the Future? The Economics of a Warming World.* New York: Zed Books.

Blau, Francine and Lawrence Kahn (2017) "The Gender Wage Gap: Extent, Trends, and Explanations," *Journal of Economic Literature*, 55(3), 789–865.

Brundtland, Gro H. (1987) "Report of the World Commission on Environment and Development: Our Common Future." United Nations General Assembly document A/42/427. Accessed 7/25/19: http://www.un-documents.net/our-common-future.pdf.

D'Alisa, Giacomo, Federico Demaria and Giorgos Kallis (2015) *Degrowth: A Vocabulary for a New Era.* London: Routledge.

Daly, Herman (2005) "Economics in A Full World," *Scientific American*, 293(3), 100–107.

Dengler, Corinna, Birte Strunk. (2018) "The Monetized Economy Versus Care and the Environment: Degrowth Perspectives on Reconciling an Antagonism," *Feminist Economics*, 24(3), 160–183.

Garver, Geoffrey and Mark S. Goldberg (2015) "Boundaries and Indicators: Conceptualizing the Measuring Progress Toward an Economy of Right Relationship Constrained by Ecological Limits," in *Ecological Economics for the Anthropocene*, Peter G. Brown and Peter Timmerman (eds.). New York: Columbia University Press, 149–189.

Goodwin, Neva, Julie Nelson and Jonathan Harris (2009) *Macroeconomics in Context.* Armonk, NY: M.E. Sharpe.

Hegewisch, Ariane and Heidi Hartmann (2019) "The Gender Wage Gap: 2018 Earnings Differences by Race and Ethnicity." Institute for Women's Policy Research. Accessed on 7/18/19: https://iwpr.org/publications/gender-wage-gap-2018/.

Jochimsen, Maren and Ulrike Knobloch (1997) "Making the Hidden Visible: The Importance of Caring Activities and Their Principles for Any Economy," *Ecological Economics*, 20, 107–112.

Keynes, John M. (1924) "Alfred Marshall: 1842–1924." In *Essays in Biography* (1933), G. Keynes (ed.) National Committee on Pay Equity. Accessed on 8/9/19: https://www.pay-equity.org/index.html.

National Oceanic and Atmospheric Administration (NOAA) (2019). "Carbon Dioxide Levels Hit Record Peak in May." *NOAA Research News.* Accessed on 8/19/19: https://research.noaa.gov/article/ArtMID/587/ArticleID/2461/Carbon-dioxide-levels-hit-record-peak-in-May.

Solow, Robert M. (1993) "Sustainability: An Economist's Perspective," in *Economics of the Environment: Selected Readings.* 3rd ed., R. Dorfman, N.S. Dorfman (eds.). New York: Norton.

Steffen, Will, Katherine Richardson, Johan Rockström, Sarah E. Cornell, Ingo Fetzer, Elena M. Bennett, Reinette Biggs, Stephen R. Carpenter, Wim de Vries, Cynthia A. de Wit, et al. (2015) "Planetary Boundaries: Guiding Human Development on a Changing Planet," *Science*, 347(6223), 736–745.

United Nations (2019) "17 Goals to Transform Our World." Accessed on 8/19/19: https://www.un.org/sustainabledevelopment/.

United Nations Statistics Division (2015) *The World's Women 2015: Trends and Statistics*. Accessed on 7/16/2019: https://unstats.un.org/unsd/gender/aboutWW2015.html.

Waring, Marilyn (1988) *If Women Counted: A New Feminist Economics*. San Francisco: Harper & Row.

Index

Page numbers in **bold** refer to figures, page numbers in *italic* refer to tables.